Men with ADHD

The Complete Guide for Organizing, Overcoming Distractions, and Strengthening Relationships. Manage Emotions and Thrive at Work and Life

Nick Johnson

&

James Smith

Table of Contents

Introduction

In all the time that we humans have spent on this planet, we have explored so much. We have even managed to explore outside of our planet. Yet, with as much as we have explored and as much knowledge as we've hoarded, the greatest mysteries we still have to solve can be found within us.

We have only scratched the surface of how the human mind works, but the amount of knowledge we have gathered is nothing less than astonishing. With this better understanding, we have been able to identify the different ways in which the human mind functions. One such different way has been named ADHD—short for *attention-deficit/hyperactivity disorder.*

For a very long time, those with ADHD have been misdiagnosed as being simply hyperactive, energetic, or just gifted. Then, as our understanding of mental health started to improve, we finally identified ADHD, as attention deficit disorder (ADD), and the diagnosis was split between those that are hyperactive and those that are not hyperactive. By 1987, these two aspects were combined, and ADD became ADHD.

Although it has been almost 40 years since ADHD was successfully identified and defined as we know it today, there is still much about it that we don't understand. Similarly, there is still a stigma attached as well—most often when it comes to men who have not only ADHD but any form of mental disorder.

In this book, we will open conversation, educate, and through tolerance and open conversation, not only help to remove the stigma attached to mental disorders but also help to increase understanding for men with ADHD on how to live with it, as well as help those around them to understand what it means.

When someone hears the term mental disorder, they immediately assume there is something wrong with the person living with it and that they are unable to function normally in society. This is simply untrue and overexaggerated. A disorder such as ADHD simply means that normal life for you will look a bit different from that of others.

Your way of doing things, your train of thought, and even your perspective on life may be vastly different. You will still, however, be able to function and achieve absolutely anything that others are able to. The road you take to get there will just differ a bit and may contain a few more stops and some extra scenery.

In this book, we'll discuss how someone with ADHD can achieve success in all aspects of their lives, from their careers to their love life and everything in between. The best place to start, however, will be in identifying whether you have ADHD or not.

CHAPTER 1

Do I Have ADHD?

Although ADHD has come to an age where it is more accepted and recognized, there are still many adults who have remained undiagnosed. As a result, there are many people that listen to others talking about ADHD and how it affects their daily lives that find it extremely relatable and wonder whether or not they may be undiagnosed as well.

I cannot diagnose you. No book or website will be able to diagnose you. However, I may be able to help you recognize the symptoms of ADHD which will allow you to feel more comfortable approaching a registered mental health practitioner that has the ability to diagnose you.

Symptoms

We've touched on the difference between ADHD and ADD earlier. The fact of the matter is that these are both the same disorder with the only difference between the two being the hyperactivity levels and the timing of the diagnosis—since the mid-2000s, ADHD has encompassed all forms of this disorder, and ADD is no longer applied as a diagnosis. According to the NHS, about two or three in every ten people with ADHD do not suffer from hyperactivity or impulsiveness. This means that you could have only inattentiveness, only hyperactivity, or in some cases both. For this reason, we'll be looking at the symptoms of both of these.

ADHD is most easily diagnosed during childhood and can be spotted when enough of the symptoms present themselves in more than one environment. The reason for this is that ADHD quite often presents as a child being bored or not being stimulated enough. This can happen very easily in any situation. Take school, for instance: If the child is not interested in the topic at hand, they could very easily become bored and stop paying attention. This could be misinterpreted as the child not being stimulated enough, but could just as easily be because this is a very difficult topic or environment for them.

However, if the child is constantly bored at school, then goes home to a place where they can choose their own stimulation, but still gets bored easily, that is a lot more likely to be ADHD.

The symptoms will present themselves as either being more inattentive or more hyperactive and impulsive. Each variation has different symptoms, and a person with ADHD will often fluctuate between either of these variations or in some cases a combination of the two.

Inattentiveness

- Difficulty maintaining focus on a specific task

- Making seemingly careless and small mistakes

- Appearing forgetful and absent-minded

- Being unable to remain engaged in tasks that do not pique their interest

- Having difficulty with listening and following direct instructions

- Frequently changing the activity or task they are busy with, without completing it

- Having difficulties with organizing tasks

Hyperactivity and Impulsiveness

- Difficulties sitting still, more specifically in surroundings that are calm or quiet

- Constantly fidgeting and moving about

- Being unable to maintain concentration on tasks

- Excessively moving around

- Excessive talking or verbal diarrhea

- Being impatient and unable to wait their turn

- Acting impulsively and without thinking

- Regularly interrupting conversations

- Having very little or no sense of danger

Adulthood

Although these symptoms mainly appear in childhood, they tend to remain well into adulthood. With the improvement of our understanding of mental health, it has even become quite common for many adults to be diagnosed with ADHD. This is done through a combination of current symptoms, as well as recognition of symptoms that were apparent during childhood. Due to the fact that these symptoms need to be identified in reverse, diagnoses in adults are still less common than diagnoses of children.

Another factor to consider is that the symptoms that are transferred into adulthood will become a lot less subtle than they were during childhood. This change can also mean that the way ADHD affects adults might look very different from how it affected them during childhood.

The following list describes symptoms that adults with ADHD will display and has been compiled by specialists in this field:

- Carelessness

- Lack of attention to detail

- Regularly beginning a new task before completing old ones

- Poor organizational skills

- Inability to remain focused

- Inability to properly prioritize tasks

- Losing and misplacing things

- Forgetfulness

- Restlessness and edginess

- Difficulty keeping quiet, and speaking out of turn

- Blurting out responses and often interrupting others

- Mood swings, irritability, and a quick temper

- Inability to deal with stress

- Extreme impatience

- Taking risks in activities, often with little or no regard for personal safety or the safety of others—for example, driving dangerously

Statistics

The statistics below are accurate as of the time of writing (December 2022). The reason I specify this is that although we understand ADHD a lot more than we did 20 years ago, our understanding of all mental health is still in its infancy. Our understanding of mental health is continuously changing in the same way that our understandings of all sciences are always changing. As a result, new information about ADHD is becoming available all the time. However, it is useful to keep in mind the general patterns of the following statistics:

- Men are three times more likely to be diagnosed than women, with about 13% of men being diagnosed with ADHD and only 4.2% of women.

- ADHD symptoms tend to appear during the ages of three to six years old, while the average age of diagnosis is at seven years old.

- In the US, roughly 4% of adults are diagnosed with ADHD.

- ADHD tends to appear less severe with age. Five-year-olds are most often the ones diagnosed with severe ADHD, while seven-year-olds tend to receive a moderate diagnosis and eight-year-olds a mild diagnosis.

- Children in a household where English is their first language are approximately four times more likely to be diagnosed than their counterparts where English is an additional language.

- Thirty-three percent of students that have been diagnosed with ADHD do not finish school. This is more than double the number of dropouts without ADHD.

- More than double the number of students with ADHD attend trade or vocational schools compared to those without ADHD.

- Nine in ten children that have been diagnosed will enjoy support or accommodation from schools.

- Ten percent of people diagnosed with ADHD will develop an addiction to substances.

- Bipolar disorder is roughly six times more common in those that have been diagnosed with ADHD.

- Only 15% of people diagnosed with ADHD will continue to complete a four-year degree at university.

- Three out of four children that have been diagnosed will receive therapy, medication, or both.

- ADHD drivers have a 47% higher chance of accidents.

- Two out of three people diagnosed with ADHD will also be diagnosed with another co-occurring condition.

- A quarter of children diagnosed with ADHD are also on the autism spectrum.

- Half of diagnosed children will also have a learning disability.

- One in ten children with ADHD will also be diagnosed with Tourette's—this is also likely to precede the ADHD diagnosis.

- Ten percent of diagnosed children will suffer from speech difficulties.

- Half of diagnosed children will also be diagnosed with oppositional defiant disorder.

- Of children diagnosed with ADHD, 25% will also be diagnosed with general behavior disorders.

- One in five people diagnosed with ADHD will also struggle with depression.

These statistics do not necessarily mention men, but they do tell us that men are a lot more likely to be diagnosed with ADHD, which in turn means that these statistics are a lot more likely to be present in men.

CHAPTER 2

Courageous Acceptance and Responsibility

Quite often—especially in men and people that are diagnosed with ADHD at a later stage of their life—acceptance is the most difficult aspect of ADHD. There is a multitude of reasons for this. The main culprit, however, is not the stigma still attached to mental health or pride but, instead, the fear we all have of not being perfect. Having ADHD does not mean that there is anything wrong with you, and it is your responsibility to build up the courage to accept it. Luckily, there is no reason you can't get some help with this.

What It Looks Like to Accept ADHD

When you get diagnosed with ADHD, especially at a young age, it doesn't really feel like anything changes. Yes, there is now a decent explanation for a lot of your behavior and how your brain works, yet it can still feel like you are disconnected from this diagnosis.

It is only when we truly understand and accept what this diagnosis means to us that it actually starts to make a difference in our lives. We no longer just see it as a diagnosis that others use to explain why we are different. Instead, we see it as having a different set of tools in our toolbox. While others may have different screwdrivers for different types of screws, we'll have one screwdriver that works on all types of screws. It might take a bit of extra work on some screws, but on other screws, it is easier to use, all you have to do is learn how to use it.

This doesn't mean you will just magically be perfectly fine. Instead, it means you'll be able to better understand both your strengths and weaknesses. You will be able to understand the best way to navigate your life. As an example, I know that my ADHD means that I will procrastinate important tasks up until the last possible moment; then, in the eleventh hour, I will suddenly find a passion that cannot be extinguished. This is when I do my best work. That is exactly what I did while writing this book. I got a deadline set up for when it should be completed and left myself with more than enough time to procrastinate and build anxiety. A few days before my deadline, that passion kicked in, and here you are seeing the end result.

This is, by far, not the healthiest nor most effective way to approach a task, but this is the way that works the best for me and in which I find myself the most productive. This is what acceptance looks like, my weaknesses are my lack of urgency, inattentiveness, failure to focus, and difficulty to initiate a task. My strengths, however, are my ability to work under pressure and my creativity which is improved by my habit of finishing my task mentally over and over while procrastinating. The latter is a good coping technique for anyone with ADHD, which we'll discuss later.

As you may have noticed from my example, acceptance is not just *knowing* that you have this condition, but truly *understanding* the condition and how it affects you, your mind, and your behavior. You will need to understand the challenges it will create in your life and then figure out how to approach these obstacles in a way that is productive for you. You also need to remember that this is a condition that affects your mind, and since each of our minds works in its own unique ways, our way of approaching them will also be unique.

I want you to focus on the following few points in particular:

- Your brain chemistry is different from those of others, accept this and that it does not mean there is anything wrong, broken, or bad about you.

- Some people are tall, and some are short. This makes different tasks and actions easier or more difficult for them, but this does not determine their entire identity.

ADHD is exactly the same.

- Regardless of your status in life, it will always have its ups and downs. There is nothing we can do to change this, we need to accept it.

- By accepting your ADHD, it does not mean that you will no longer have stress and difficulties—those will remain. You will, however, change how you engage with yourself.

To truly accept our diagnosis, we need to understand what is happening to us and how it affects us. We'll be looking into this through the course of the next few chapters, but first, we need to start by understanding acceptance. To do so, we'll be looking at the various stages of acceptance next.

Stages of Acceptance

Receiving any type of permanent diagnosis is a life-changing event similar to trauma. Your brain needs to accept that it will forever need to deal with this new information and change its life accordingly. This is not an easy feat, and although some of us might be able to go through the process a bit faster than others, you still need to allow your mind to process this in its own way and on its own time.

The following are the stages of acceptance that you will most likely go through while accepting your diagnosis. Some people might skip a step or two, others might switch steps around, that is all perfectly fine, the important thing is to accept it.

Freedom

Freedom is normally the first feeling you have after receiving your diagnosis. You finally feel better about everything that went wrong in your life. All the times you found it impossible to focus on a task, could not stick to a deadline, or struggled to sit still for longer than five seconds, all make sense now. You were not just lazy or less intelligent or whatever else you thought was wrong with you. By finally having an answer, you can see the solution in front of you—you feel positive and happy.

Anger

With this freedom, you start to analyze your life; you look at all those little moments in your past and start to focus on every little detail. This is when you begin to realize that these events occurred quite often and appeared very similar in nature. You also realize that the same people were always present, that they were aware of every situation and every symptom you had—people like your parents, siblings, teachers, and anyone else who, in your mind, was a responsible person that should have seen the symptoms and be able to identify and help you.

The important thing to remember here is that mental health is a field that is always being researched and improved upon. You could read this book today, and by next week, we could have so much new information that Noah himself may just as well have written this book on the Ark. When you presented these symptoms, those around you may not have been educated to know exactly what it points to.

Grief—"I Wish I Knew Sooner"

This is the most normal next step for adults. The later in life you get diagnosed, the stronger this stage will feel to you. With every example of your ADHD that impacted your life, you will wish that you had known back then. Your mind will keep saying that if only you had been diagnosed before that event, it could have been avoided, your life could have been so much different, and you could have achieved so much more.

You will need to realize that we will never know what could have been or what would have worked out for the better if things had happened differently. It is perfectly natural to want to have known sooner, the important thing is to not get stuck in that mindset. We can't change the past, but we can influence the future.

Education

This is, again, a natural step following the "I wish I knew sooner" stage. You start to wonder why nobody knew anything sooner and what else you are currently missing. This leads you to seek education on the topic. You might even have bought this book due to being in this stage. It is a great stage to be in, even more of your life and actions start to make sense, and you are preparing yourself for the rest of your life.

Self-Loathing

Although you become more prepared and more educated, this could all start to feel overwhelming. The thought that stayed in my mind was, "Nobody else has to research how to use their minds." The dark and negative thoughts start to seep through, and you start to think that there is something wrong with you.

These are all completely normal feelings. It is best to reassure yourself that you are not the first nor the last person to feel this way. In fact, so many people who do not ever get diagnosed with any disorder or condition will go through these exact feelings at some stage in their life. As humans, we are not designed to be perfect; we all have our own set of strengths, weaknesses, faults, and skills.

You are *not* broken, you are *not* a failure, and you are *not* in any situation that cannot be saved. The faster you realize and accept this, the faster you will be able to move past this stage of your overall acceptance.

Denial

Much like with grief and trauma, you will likely also enter the denial stage. This is when you start to wonder if the treatment you've been prescribed is making things better or worse. You begin to ask whether or not you actually have ADHD; does ADHD even exist?

This stage does the most harm to you, as it gets you to ignore all the progress and education you have gotten so far. When taking medication or using techniques and mechanisms to better cope with your ADHD, there will always be side effects. These side effects will not always be positive, and in fact, in the short term, they can appear to do more harm than good. This means that when you stop your treatment, you will see these negative side effects drop away, as they are visible and obvious, yet the less visible and less obvious long-term benefits will go unnoticed.

You might feel good in the moment, but a week, a month, or ten years later, you will finally realize what you lost. The best way to get through this stage and move on is by leaning on those close to you. In fact, as soon as you start doing this, you will already start entering the next stage.

Community-Seeking

When you start to move out of the denial stage and acknowledge your diagnosis once again, you will start to feel lonely. You will need someone who is going through the same experience as you—somebody who you can discuss side effects and techniques with. This will be the last stage in your acceptance journey, as this means that you will have to make peace with your diagnosis and treatment in order to share and discuss it with others.

A community is not necessarily a group of people that meet regularly, in fact, your community can consist of podcasts, media personalities such as Connor DeWolfe, or even groups on social media. The one thing you should look out for in your community is that those you interact with and from whom you receive information are well-educated and that they share accurate and correct information.

Your community should be a positive influence and not cause more damage to your mental health.

CHAPTER 3

What's Been Going On in Your Head

Ignorance breeds contempt, but knowledge breeds acceptance. –Anonymous

Education is one part of the acceptance journey. It is also one of the most important aspects of living with any type of condition. We need to understand exactly how ADHD is affecting our mind, which will allow us to understand how to approach and treat this condition, as well as open conversations regarding our condition.

The Neuroscience of ADHD

Your brain is constantly creating a very wide variety of chemicals and hormones that it uses to control your entire body, from the physical all the way to your emotions. This is how you obtain feelings connected to your emotions, maintain focus, and even process your senses.

ADHD is the first disorder that was identified as being the result of a deficiency in a neurotransmitter—specifically norepinephrine, in this case. In less technical terms, your brain is constantly sending signals from one area to another in the form of these chemicals such as norepinephrine. When you have ADHD, this means that your body is unable to send these chemicals in the way that it is supposed to.

The importance of norepinephrine is that the brain creates it out of a molecule called L-DOPA. Your brain turns L-DOPA into dopamine before it becomes norepinephrine. Dopamine might sound familiar to you, and this would be because it is more commonly called "the happy chemical." This is the neurotransmitter that is responsible for making you feel good. Of course, the ways that these chemicals interact with certain parts of your brain mean that the brain itself is not solely responsible for making you feel good and happy. We'll be taking a look at how norepinephrine interacts with several important areas of your brain and what these assist you in.

The four areas of your brain discussed below are always in constant communication with each other, which means that if there is a deficiency in just one of these areas, it will still have an impact on the other areas.

Frontal Cortex

The frontal cortex of the brain is the region that controls your executive functioning, which allows you to plan, start, and complete complex tasks; remain attentive to the task at hand; and successfully organize. When we don't receive the required norepinephrine to this area of the brain, these are the actions that we will struggle with doing the most.

Limbic System

Your limbic system is responsible for your emotions. This area requires norepinephrine to stabilize your emotions and to regulate the correct emotions at the correct times—for example, to make sure you actually feel good enough when you are happy. When your limbic system does not receive the adequate chemicals, you are more prone to feelings of depression, anxiety, and sudden shifts in your moods. This is why ADHD is often accompanied by behavioral difficulties.

Basal Ganglia

The basal ganglia are your brain's communication center. All information in your brain passes through this area. Think about what happens if a call center does not receive enough power. Some calls won't go through, others will be cut off every time power is lost; radio messages will only come through when there is power and cut out when the power goes off, which means you'll only receive part of those messages, and anyone attempting to use a computer will most probably be unable to finish their task and have to constantly restart these tasks. Now, imagine this call center is supposed to receive information from each of these calls in order to be able to make a decision. When the information they receive is incomplete, the decision will still have to be made and may look irrational to someone from the outside. This effect is why someone with ADHD will often seem to be impulsive, disorganized, and inattentive. It is simply a case of their communication center not working as it is supposed to.

Reticular Activating System

The reticular activating system forms the main pathways in and out of your brain. You can think of this system as a turnstile in a train station. However, it sometimes gets stuck, causing a line to build up for people both entering and exiting. Once in a while, this means that a whole lot of people start moving, and at other times, there is no movement at all. In the brain, this effect is what causes hyperactivity, failure to maintain attention, and impulsive choices.

Brain Chemistry

ADHD is believed to be mainly hereditary, which means that it finds its cause through certain genes transferred by one's parents. However, this is still the subject of some debate as there are some cases that do not appear to be hereditary; in these cases, the cause of ADHD is thought to be connected to a variety of other issues such as difficult pregnancies, prenatal exposure to substances, premature delivery, low birth weight, excessively high body lead levels, or a postnatal injury to the prefrontal area of your brain. In essence, this means that anyone is susceptible to ADHD. A parent can take whatever steps they can think of to ensure a perfect pregnancy, but something going wrong during birth could lead to ADHD.

There is still a major misconception that ADHD is caused by unhealthy sugar intake, excessive technology indulgence, social or environmental influences such as being bullied in school, an unstable family life, or even poor parenting. The truth is that there is no evidence that any of these could be a causing factor of ADHD. Instead, these factors could aggravate preexisting ADHD.

ADHD, much like other behavioral mental health conditions, is caused by an imbalance in the brain chemistry, which means that behavioral issues are a result of ADHD, not a cause of it.

Chapter 4

Embrace Your Emotional
Regulation

We've already covered the fact that ADHD impacts your ability to regulate and stabilize your emotions and moods. In the modern society that we live in, it is more acceptable for men to actually have and show emotions, which is a great thing. The problem, however, is that we still need to prove that we are in fact in control of our emotions and not the other way around.

I want to take a moment here and address the stigma that we men face when it comes to emotions and mental health. The purpose of this book is to help men realize that we too are only human and that we don't always need to be perfect. Feeling emotions and having mental health struggles, do *not* make us weak or any less equipped to be there for our families. This is quite often the reason that men refrain from seeking a diagnosis and, even more seriously, treatment.

I would like to reassure you that accepting and acknowledging your mental health and emotions are in fact a strength that will help you to more effectively be there for those around you. You can only be strong enough to lift a mountain off someone else when you have trained by lifting the mountain off yourself.

Patience and Courage

Patience and courage go together hand-in-hand. Being courageous means having patience, and having patience means being courageous enough to wait. For someone with ADHD, these are often the most difficult emotions to process and maintain.

Patience

When it comes to having patience, it means that we need to remain calm and attentive. Yet, a person with ADHD tends to be a lot more impatient, hyperactive, and impulsive than their neurotypical peers. This is one of the largest obstacles that we need to learn how to overcome. How do we remain patient when we are so bored that we physically become agitated when we have to wait for something? Or when we become so excited that our body has no way of remaining still?

The Cleveland Clinic has provided us with seven tips for improving our patience:

- **Mindfulness:** The trick of this tip is to just observe. Be mindful of your surroundings as well as yourself. Start by focusing on your breathing and nothing else. It won't take long for your focus to start drifting, let it do so for a moment and see where it goes. Once you have observed what is pulling your attention, shift it back to your breathing.

- **Accept your circumstances:** Accept what is happening around you. I don't want you to try and change it, simply accept it. This might be something as simple as just acknowledging that you are waiting in a line and that it will take you another hour to get to the front of it. A very important aspect of this tip is that you stop wondering how long it will take the line to move, stop asking yourself when the person in front will be done, and stop wondering how long it will take them. Just accept that you are indeed in this line and that it will take a long time.

- **Force discomfort on yourself:** When you are bitten by a mosquito, how do you treat this bite? It itches like crazy, and all you want to do is scratch that itch. Yet, with every scratch, it just becomes worse. It's only when you leave it to itch that it starts to heal itself. Impatience can be healed in a similar way. By allowing someone to cut in line or by resisting the impulse of doing something that you are not yet ready for, you will start to build a tolerance for that feeling you get within yourself when you become impatient.

- **Slow down:** Force yourself to take a breath and slow down. When you feel yourself being anxious while running at full speed, the answer is not always to run faster. Instead, it may be to change gears, conserve your fuel, and travel at a more economic pace. ADHD means that when we get ourselves to move, we do so at the speed of light. This, in turn, means that we tend to make a decision before we allow all the information to be absorbed and processed. By forcing ourselves to slow down a bit, we also force ourselves to be less impulsive.

- **Playtime:** Remember that ADHD means we have a lack of the chemical dopamine. Luckily, we can create our own dopamine. By doing things that we love, we force our brain to release this dopamine. So, don't be afraid to take a step away every once in a while to just sing, dance, play a game, or do anything else that makes you feel good before returning to the task at hand. When you are waiting in a line, hum a song you love to yourself. Release the dopamine, and you will find that your patience will show an increase.

- **Wait before you fix it:** Remember that it not only takes time for your ADHD mind to process all the information at hand but that some of the information might not get processed at all. This means that when you complete a task or look at a situation, you might feel that it is broken, incomplete, or just not right. When you feel like this, you might attempt to fix it, and in doing so, only make it worse. This is why it is important to give it a moment, and fully allow yourself enough time to reassess the situation before you attempt to fix what seems broken.

- **Listen:** A situation in which we often find our ADHD causing us to become sidetracked is during conversations, especially when someone else is attempting to tell us a story. This is why this tip is to force yourself to listen and pay attention to what someone else is telling you. Instead of starting to plan your response as soon as the other person starts speaking, try to analyze each aspect of their conversation. Focus on the words and tone of another, and increase your understanding of their meaning. This will make the conversation more interesting for you and allow you to remain patient within this conversation.

Courage

We've already established that courage and patience work together, let me explain why. Someone with ADHD has their mind always racing at 1,000 miles per second. This means that— especially when we receive a major influx of adrenaline and energy—our brains make impulsive decisions at a fast rate even with little information.

Quite often, this leads us to become paralyzed by the choices we have available to us or for us to choose the flight response element of the fight-or-flight mechanism. This doesn't make you a coward, it simply means that your brain has thought of so many possibilities that it either cannot decide what course of action will be the best to obtain the preferred outcome or has decided that the outcome is too uncertain, making it seem that removing yourself from the situation has the highest chance of prompting a safe and positive outcome for you.

There is also the issue of confrontation: When your brain cannot process information in a satisfactory way and cannot regulate your emotions as it should, it is only natural for you to become scared of confrontation. Your brain realizes that this is a high-stress situation that it might just not be wired to deal with as effectively as you would like it to.

Luckily, there are a few ways for us to become more courageous. These tips could also be used to help you face your diagnosis:

- **Acknowledgment:** You will never be able to be courageous in the face of your fears if you refuse to acknowledge that they exist. By ignoring your fears, you are only kicking the can down the road to be faced at a later stage. By acknowledging them, you are saying that you are ready to face them.

- **Confrontation:** Face your fears. It might sound like a tired old cliche, but it is still sound advice. I don't mean you should necessarily jump into a pit of snakes just because you are scared of snakes, but perhaps, ask yourself why you are scared of snakes. Even just realizing that a fear is irrational can be enough to help you overcome choice paralysis and your flight reaction when you find yourself coming face-to-face with it.

- **Talk yourself up:** Positive self-reinforcement can be a huge asset. When you hear that critic that lives in your head telling you that you are not good enough or that you did something wrong, shut it down by killing it with kindness. We often find that our fears are rooted in our own insecurities. This is especially true for men with ADHD. When you think that you are weak or broken, you will lack the confidence that you need in order to succeed with your ADHD.

- **Create brave habits:** Since our fear is often rooted within our ADHD, creating a habit of being courageous can often be the answer we require. If you place yourself in a situation on a regular basis, you will feel more comfortable when you are in a similar situation. For example, going on a roller coaster regularly will help you to become used to the feeling of heights and high speeds, so next time you end up being in a car that is slipping on a wet road or need to cross a very high bridge, you may feel more comfortable acting while in experiencing the same amount of fear.

- **Mindfulness:** This is another tip that goes hand-in-hand with patience. When you are constantly assessing and observing the world around you, you allow your mind a greater amount of time to process information. When your fear sensations kick in, you will only need to process the actual event since you will have already processed the environment.

- **Mentorship:** A mentor is more than just somebody to teach you something, it is someone that has already gone through the experiences you are about to face or, alternatively, has more knowledge that can be used to help guide you. This is why a mentor can be a very powerful asset in any situation, but especially for someone with ADHD. Seeing another man that has managed to get their life on track and become successful, while also being diagnosed with ADHD, will not only prove to you that you can do so as well but also enable you to access their advice on how to do the same.

- **Fail:** Our largest fear in life is quite often the fear of failure. Have you ever tried to build a shed, create some pottery, or even paint something? Many people will never do something like this because they believe that they do not possess the correct skills and talents, a belief that is often reinforced after trying it once and failing. However, we need to fail once in a while in order to learn from our mistakes.

Stop fearing failure, but instead, accept and embrace it as a moment of education.

- **Embrace imperfections:** Remember that there is no such thing as a perfect human, so if humanity itself is not perfect, then how can we expect everything we do to be perfect? When we stop judging ourselves by whether we've achieved perfection or not, our fear of failure also lowers immediately. When this is out of the way, we finally realize that we can do something for no reason other than curiosity and experience.

Learn to Self-Monitor

Another very useful way of embracing your emotional regulation is by continuously checking on yourself, your emotions, and your state of mind. This is called *self-monitoring*. A person who is seen to excel at self-monitoring or engage in acquisitive self-monitoring is someone who will constantly change their own behavior according to the demands of their social environment. Whereas a person that struggles with self-monitoring or engages only in protective self-monitoring will allow their own needs and feelings to wholly determine their behavior.

Much like everything else in life, self-monitoring requires

balance. It is unhealthy to constantly focus on your own needs and emotions, but at the same time completely ignoring them is also very unhealthy.

Perfect self-monitoring involves knowing when you should engage in acquisitive self-monitoring and when you should engage in protective self-monitoring. During events or situations that require a lot of social interaction, such as a party or meeting a stranger, acquisitive self-monitoring would be the best course of action, as it will best allow you to participate in a social event. Contrastingly, when you are around your spouse or other close family members the best course of action will be protective self-monitoring, as this allows you to be more in tune with your inner experience and tend to your own needs without seeming rude or selfish.

There are three easy steps to learning to self-monitor:

1. **Identify:** Determine what behavior needs to change and how you want to change this behavior in yourself. This could be something like talking less in a social setting because you feel like you have verbal diarrhea or speaking more because you feel like you are socially awkward and never engage with others in a social setting. This could also, of course, extend to other aspects of your life such as eating habits, exercise, and most importantly, how you deal with your moods.

2. **Record:** The next step you want to take is to start making

note of your reactions and behaviors that occur in the situations you have identified to be changed. These can be mental notes, physical notes, or even entries on an app, and may involve something like writing down every time you feel a shift in your emotions and how you acted to return your emotions to where you wanted them. After a while, you will be able to see a trend as to when these behaviors occur, whether they have increased or decreased in frequency since you have attempted to make a change, and what changes work.

3. **Schedule:** The most important aspect of self-monitoring is continuously checking in on yourself. We tend to ignore habits of self-improvement in favor of keeping up with modern life, but in doing so, we stop the improvement altogether. This is why a schedule is so important. It will help you to ensure that you keep up with your self-monitoring. This schedule doesn't have to be extremely strict. It could be as simple as just checking in after specific events or just checking in every few days regarding a variety of different situations and events.

Tend to Your Physical Health

Your physical health is tied directly to your mental health. When your body is healthy, energetic, and in good shape, you feel good about yourself, and you have energy to face every day. A major part of physical health is exercise, which allows you to rid yourself of excess energy and let your mind rest.

To keep your physical health in step you can follow these tips:

- **Track your weight:** By keeping a record of your weight, you will know when it changes. You can use this record as a roadmap to your physical health. By ensuring that your weight stays at a healthy figure, you will ensure that you know how to adjust your eating and exercising habits. A sudden increase or decrease in weight can also be indicative of stress or other health factors. However, keep in mind that you are concerned with overall trends. Daily fluctuations in weight are to be expected and should not become a source of anxiety.

- **Eat better:** What and when we consume does not just impact our weight. Having regular and healthy meals throughout the day ensures that your body constantly has the required nutrients to ensure that you have enough energy for the entire day. Keeping your gut healthy also helps with the production of neurotransmitters, enabling you to more easily manage your ADHD symptoms and all the required interactions you will engage in.

- **Take supplements:** Contrary to popular beliefs, multivitamin supplements do not necessarily help you to heal faster or prevent diseases. However, this doesn't mean that there are no benefits to taking supplements. It is especially helpful to take these supplements when your diet might be lacking in fruits and vegetables.

- **Drink water:** The most natural drink that any of us can have is water. Your body is made out of 70% water—a very valuable resource that is utilized by every part of your body. When you do not take in enough water, you not only become dehydrated and lose energy, but your entire body starts to shut down—even your digestive system slows down which, in turn, will cause weight gain.

- **Exercise:** You don't need to join a gym, get a personal trainer, or do anything that hectic. Just taking a stroll in the evenings or doing a home workout can be enough to improve your general health. As mentioned earlier, physical exercise carries huge benefits for you. At the very least, it allows you time to get away from the stress and constant engagement of your daily life, giving you time to think and settle your emotions.

- **Have less screen time:** When we are on our phones, watching tv, playing games, or even working on a computer, we tend to do so for prolonged times while sitting down and not being active. Aside from that, it has been proven that social media addictions are very negative for our mental state of mind. A simple change—such as waiting an hour before accessing technology when you wake up or taking a stroll around the room you are in every 20 minutes while having screen time—can help to improve not only your physical health but also your mental health.

- **Regulate sleep cycles:** By ensuring that you receive a good amount of sleep every night, you allow your mind time to regenerate and process the information that it had been introduced to during the course of the day. At the same time, you replenish much-needed energy.

- **Limit mind-altering substances:** There is nothing better than having a beer while watching the game or a whiskey before bed at night. This is perfectly fine, in moderation. Substances such as alcohol, nicotine, and where legal, marijuana, all have a form of influence on your body and mental health. In small amounts, the consumption of these substances is acceptable; however, overdoing it will cause definite harm.

- **Track yourself:** Most phones already come with an app that tracks your exercise and movement during the day. These are made more accurate and can track more activities with the addition of a smartwatch. Using these technologies to track your fitness journey, sleep cycle, and activities during the day will help you to stay up-to-date with your physical health.

Stay Grounded

Think of a tree that is swaying in the wind. The deeper its roots are planted, the stronger the winds it can withstand. The same applies to us. The more grounded we are in life, the more emotionally stable we remain, and the more we can deal with in life.

Here are some techniques for remaining grounded:

- **Meditation:** Believe me, I know: Meditation sounds so overdone and cliche. Meanwhile, sitting alone on the floor with some odd sounds playing around you is not just boring, it is next to impossible. Meditation, however, does have its benefits. It might take a while to get into meditation, but after a few sessions and perhaps a few guided meditation classes, you'll soon realize that meditation can help you to process information and to make peace with your emotions.

- **Immediate moments:** One of the best ways to remain grounded is to focus on the current moment and environment around you. When you are focusing on what is actually happening around you, you stop your mind from wandering and overthinking. This is also an amazing technique for someone suffering from anxiety and panic attacks. The best way to combat a panic attack is by looking for the following:

  ○ Five things you can see

- ○ Four things you can touch

- ○ Three things you can hear

- ○ Two things you can smell

- ○ One thing you can taste

- **Just breathe:** Breathing techniques are wonderful for helping you to calm down and ground yourself. When anxiety and emotions overtake us, the first thing that usually happens is that we start breathing faster, normally to the point of hyperventilating. By taking control of your breathing and slowing it down again, you will also be able to calm your emotions and feelings.

- **Nature:** Sometimes, all we need is to get away from the world that we live in. A camping or fishing trip might just be exactly what you need. This allows you to spend time away from what causes you stress, long enough to process the stress you already have. That is amplified by the beauty and calmness of nature.

Question Unhelpful Thoughts

One of the biggest challenges that men with ADHD often face is our own inner critic that tries to break us down. This inner critic is the source of the thoughts that might tell us having a mental health condition makes us less masculine, that being depressed from time to time makes us weak, or that being unable to remain focused on a task for an extended period of time makes us ill-equipped to provide for our families. These thoughts are *lying* to us.

The best way to combat these thoughts is to ask the following questions:

- **How true is this?** When you have one of these negative thoughts jump into your head—especially those that break you down and belittle you—ask yourself how much of this thought holds actual truth.

- **What makes me sure this is true?** When you have answered the first question, you need to justify it. You should almost be investigating yourself. When you have a negative thought that you believe to be true, explain to yourself why you think so. What evidence do you have to prove this? Would the people who are the closest to you agree with you?

- **What will happen if I continue to believe this thought?** When you ask yourself this question, I want you to start searching deep within yourself. Be completely honest, and think further. Start to look at every path in front of you. If you believe this negative thought, what path will it send you down? Will it stop you from achieving a dream? Will it make your life more difficult? Is the path it is sending you down the correct path?

- **How can I turn this thought around?** The best way to get rid of a negative thought is to turn it into something positive. Sometimes, just having this negative thought can already be a positive thing, as it means you don't have an inflated ego and could actually be honest and open with yourself. Unfortunately, however, it is far more likely that your inner critic is simply using this belief to berate you. As a result, you will still always need to look at these thoughts and ask yourself what you can do to make them better for yourself.

Add Uplifting Activities to Your Schedule

It is quite common for us to feel better about other aspects of our lives when we have succeeded in a seemingly different aspect altogether. The reason for this is that our brains release all the chemicals required to feel good when we succeed, and this includes dopamine—something an ADHD brain lacks.

For this reason, adding an activity to your schedule that makes you feel successful and happy can help you to feel better about your life in general and, in turn, even help you succeed with other activities that you would normally struggle with.

These could be activities such as painting, dance lessons, DIY classes, and so much more. By improving your skills or creating something—especially before you are scheduled for a tedious and mundane task—you can fool your brain into ensuring that it receives the right amount of norepinephrine, resulting in the previously mentioned areas of your brain functioning at greater efficiency.

These activities also don't necessarily have to be physical activities, they can also be any activity that you enjoy and walk away from feeling good. A round of your favorite video game, watching a game of your favorite sport, or maybe even just a drive around the block in your car all have the potential to uplift you, and when you are uplifted, your entire life feels easier.

Think Before You Act

Living with ADHD means that we are more impulsive than other people. It is not uncommon for this impulsivity to result in us making poor decisions that make us feel negative later on.

This is why it is so important for us to think before we act, no matter how difficult it is for us. Try to realistically predict what the outcome of your actions would be before you make your move. If possible, take some time away from the situation that requires you to act, and come back later when you have had time to make a proper decision.

If you find yourself in a situation where you cannot take time away before making a decision, verbalize your choices. When you verbalize your choices, even just to yourself, you are already allowing your brain to think more clearly than if you keep the conversation internal. If there is someone else you can discuss these choices with, you might find that having counsel can help you think and make a better decision.

CHAPTER 5

Exercises to Strengthen Your Self-Esteem

As we've discussed, for men with ADHD, our largest obstacle is usually our own inner critic and self-esteem. Although we have discussed a few possible ways to address this, I think that it is time we look specifically at our self-esteem and how to improve it in more depth.

Healthier Perspectives

The first step in improving your own self-esteem is to change the way that you look at yourself. Think of yourself as a coin, if you always stare at it from one side, you'll only see the head, but turn it over or walk around, and you'll see the other side of the coin. The following methods will help you to learn how to change your perspective to a healthier one:

- **Reframing thoughts:** When we look at a task before us,

it's easy to think of it in a negative way. Take mowing the lawn for example, there is a very small amount of people that actually look forward to spending hours in the sun walking up and down with a noisy engine in front of you. So, when you are thinking of doing this task, your thought might be something along the lines of, "Ugh, I have to go mow the lawn now." We want to change this to the point that you say, "I'm so happy I get to mow the lawn today." It sounds very pretentious, but just reframing how you think of something—seeing the grass as a symbol of how much you do for your family and seeing this task as yet another chance to do something for your family, like giving them a lawn to play on and a house to be proud of—will, in fact, help you feel more motivated and focused.

- **A positive monologue:** That voice inside your head absolutely loves focusing on the negatives. When you put a shirt on in the morning, that voice might tell you that your belly is way too big or that your shirt is fitting far too tight. Especially when these thoughts are untrue, we need to change them. You need to get into the habit of having more positive than negative thoughts. When you pass a mirror, make a habit of finding at least two things that you can compliment yourself on. Another trick to turning your inner monologue more positive is to start your day with a series of affirmations.

- **Walk in another's shoes:** The best way to get a healthier perspective is to get a completely new perspective. Especially in times of anger directed at another person, the most effective way to deal with these emotions is to place yourself in the shoes of a neutral party and those of the opposite party. By doing this, you could see your own mistakes much more easily, as well as show more empathy towards your fellow people. It could also help you to more easily see a possible solution than you would have if you remained viewing the situation solely from your own perspective.

- **The bigger picture:** Looking at a single task or event on its own can easily make us negative. When we focus on the smallest of problems, this problem will look larger than it actually is. Think of it as zooming in on a specific object in a photograph, when you are zoomed in that object will cover the entire screen, and to the outside, it may look like that object is the entire picture. If you zoom out and look at the true, entire picture, that object might fade into the background or become so unimportant in the grand scheme of things that you barely notice it. The same concept applies to life: Instead of focusing on a single event or task, you should rather focus on what this event or task will lead to and the eventual end result of your actions.

- **Does it spark joy?** We have all heard about the method of improving your life by removing everything that does not bring you any joy. This is actually a very good method to bring positivity to your life, and it doesn't need to be restricted to objects and clutter. By simply reassessing your social media, the news you consume, and any other aspect of your life, you can remove what makes you negative and keep the positive around you. The same can be applied to people. If you feel drained and negative after every time you are around a specific person, it might be a very good idea to stop spending time with that person and, instead, start spending time with people that make you feel positive and better with each interaction.

- **Do something good:** Is it selfish to do a good deed if you do it only to help yourself? It doesn't matter. A good deed is a good deed as long as it really helps someone in need. The reward you get from doing a good deed is that feeling of positivity and pride in yourself. It also helps you see that life can be much worse and that you can survive through a lot more. If you walk away thankful for what you have and feeling fulfilled, having made someone else's life just a little better without making them feel worse or embarrassed, and without having used this good deed to get attention and praise, then it can't truly be selfish, and in fact, it would be a very healthy way of bringing positivity to the world.

Identifying Components for a Meaningful Life

The best way of changing your perspective in life to a more

positive one is to find a meaning for your life. This is something almost all of us struggle with. Normally, people find their meaning through religion, but this is not the only way. Meaning can be found in every life and, sometimes, in the most unexpected of places.

Here are a few ways to help you find meaning in your life:

- **Find your passion:** When you have the flame of passion burning inside of you, you will easily find the motivation to keep going forward in life. Aside from motivation, your passion can also help you to form bonds with those that share your passion. In finding what makes you feel passionate, you would have already taken the first step towards finding meaning in your life. Your passion may very well give you a purpose and a goal to achieve.

- **Build relationships:** We cannot walk through life alone. By building and maintaining relationships with those around you, there is a very good chance that you will not only find meaning but also the help needed to accomplish this meaning in your life. When you share your passions with others, they can also help you to foster and grow these passions, especially when they share them.

- **Check your mood:** It is difficult to see any purpose or meaning in life when you are constantly bombarded by negative moods and emotions. We've already covered how to keep your mood and emotions in check, as well as why it is important. This is important enough that it justifies being reiterated.

- **Control your environment:** When you are in control of your environment and it is cultivated to be a positive and motivating environment, your feelings of meaningfulness will be improved. Your environment can be controlled through a variety of methods such as schedules and routines and by keeping your environment neat and tidy.

Don't Let Your ADHD Define You

When we receive a medical diagnosis such as ADHD, bipolar disorder, or any other such permanent condition, it is easy to let this take over our life. It almost becomes our entire identity. We are no longer known as the individual person we are; instead, we become just another person with ADHD.

This only succeeds in making us more negative and causing us to become stuck in our own minds. When we cannot escape from our diagnosis and are constantly reminded of it, we end up questioning our every action and thought. You start to wonder whether you will be able to finish a task or whether your ADHD will take over and prohibit you. You wonder whether or not this new interest is truly an interest, or just a new temporary hyperfixation brought upon you by your ADHD.

In order to ensure that our ADHD does not completely take over our lives and force negativity upon us, we need to actively ensure that we live a life away from this diagnosis. There is no step-by-step guide for you to follow to not let this define you, but instead, this is a journey you need to take for yourself.

You need to treat your ADHD in the same way you would treat having a cut on your hand. The only difference is that while the cut on your hand will eventually fully heal, your ADHD can only be treated. You will, however, learn how to live with it.

One of the best ways to not let your ADHD define you is by not sharing your diagnosis with just anyone. I don't want you to feel like you should hide the fact that you have ADHD, as this would be the same as denying it. Instead, ensure that you do not share this information with someone unless it is necessary or you trust them enough to share such a part of yourself with them.

Facing Challenges Effectively

When we face challenges in life and find we are unable to manage them as we are supposed to, we end up feeling negative about ourselves and can be quite unhappy that we were ill-prepared. The best way to ensure that the challenges we are guaranteed to face in our lives do not get us down is by preparing for them and facing them directly. The following preparations can be made to ensure that you face challenges effectively:

- **Plan:** There is no way to plan for each and every challenge that will cross your path, but—especially for those of us with ADHD—it can be hugely helpful to at least plan for some of the challenges that most often cross our paths. We know that we often struggle with concentration and deadlines, so ensuring that we have time scheduled to complete our work and that we will be cut off from any and all distractions is just one way that we can plan for this exact type of challenge. This concept can be applied to any challenges that we can foresee and will help to make these types of challenges easier.

- **Do not suffer alone:** No matter what challenge you face, you can take comfort in knowing that you are most definitely not the first person to go through this challenge, nor are you the last, and you are most probably not going through it alone. Just knowing that you are not alone can provide you with some form of comfort that gives you the courage to continue facing these challenges. Moreover, turning to the wider community of men with ADHD can also help you find empathetic emotional support in times of hardship.

- **Ask for help:** Once you know that you are not alone, you should feel a lot more comfortable asking for help from those around you. We often feel ashamed if we think that we cannot overcome an obstacle on our own, but this is nothing more than pride getting in our way. Never be scared to ask for and accept assistance from those around you. Remember that even though you may feel some shame getting help, you will feel so much more pride when you are asked for and can offer assistance of your own.

- **Allow your emotions:** When you are using energy to mask and hide away your emotions, you lack the energy to focus on the challenges before you. However, when you allow yourself to feel and accept these emotions, you not only have more energy for these obstacles, but you also allow yourself to process these obstacles, which will, in turn, enable you to gain a healthier perspective on them.

- **Don't give up:** It's easy to get demotivated by failure. You can even get demotivated by an obstacle that appears to be very difficult. The key is to keep going. Perseverance is key here. You will always fail at what you refuse to attempt, but if you keep trying, keep practicing, and never give up, you will succeed.

- **Work smarter instead of harder:** There is always more than one way to complete a task, and often, the most well-known way is not the best way to do it. Before you take any action and start with a task or obstacle, take a moment to contemplate the different ways of approaching this obstacle. Then, decide which way would work best for you.

CHAPTER 6

ADHD Does Not Limit Your Career

One of the biggest fears surrounding this condition is that having ADHD means that you will be unable to access some career paths. The thinking is that careers that require a lot of mental energy and mundane tasks—such as corporate work—will be impossible for us to do, as our minds will wander too easily, and we would get bored. Instead, people with ADHD often find themselves working trade jobs in which they are physically engaged the entire time. The short of it all is that this is completely untrue, and anyone with ADHD can do any type of job, especially if they find this job to be a part of their passions.

Losing the Fear

The first step we need to take is to get rid of our fears that we can't do whatever job we want to. The fact of ADHD is that you function better when you follow the activities that release dopamine within you. As covered previously, your happy chemicals help you to function more easily. So, when you follow your passion or find yourself in a work environment that makes you happy, that will make it a lot easier for you to follow that career.

Easier does not always mean easy, however. In fact, it normally just means less difficult. So, why am I telling you this? It's simple: An ADHD brain means that you will most probably hyperfixate on the points that worry you, and if your ADHD presents anything like mine, that means you won't let it go until you have very clearly covered every aspect of this point from both an emotional and logical perspective. This means that you should have both the positive and negative aspects laid out before you.

The negative is that even when you enjoy your job, you will have difficult days. Regardless of which career you pursue, there will be aspects of it that won't interest or stimulate you. The trick here is to use the happy chemicals of the parts that you do enjoy to carry you through the parts that you don't.

It is, however, within the negativity that the positivity can be found. You would not put up with the negativity if it did not bring some sort of positivity. That means that even if you are in a career only to ensure you can survive, have a roof over your head, and put food on your table, there is still some positivity to see. So, when you are feeling negative, think about paying your rent just before you have to do a specifically difficult task. The feeling of satisfaction from achieving a goal or completing a task will help you to function during this task. This positivity doesn't need to come from a mundane task such as paying your rent; whatever releases your dopamine is your golden key.

In the end, all you need to remember is that when you follow your passion, even outside of work hours, nothing is out of your abilities.

Matching Your Strengths and Interests

Although there is nothing off limits to you, it is still better to match your strengths and interests with each other. This entails taking a very close look at your ADHD and how it presents itself.

Generally, people with ADHD do well in high-paced and high-stress environments. Being first responders, emergency room workers, athletes, journalists, retail workers, and teachers are career paths that are generally a good fit for those of us with ADHD. This is because these careers tend to agree with hyperactivity. Before you are required to focus on the same task, the same person, or even the same object for too long, something new will come along that requires your attention.

Yet, since ADHD presents differently in each individual—meaning that although the majority of people with ADHD present with hyperactivity and short attention spans, not everyone does—you will need to assess yourself. Write down all your strengths and weaknesses, each and every aspect of your personality such as what you find easier to focus on, what activities you enjoy, when you have energy, and when you do not. When you have all this written down, start looking at each of your possible career choices, and analyze the possible ways that you can use these aspects of yourself to help you in these possible careers.

When you have identified what strengths you have and connected them to your interests, you already have a basic game plan set out. It's also natural to find out that creating this list will make it align with your passions, even if you didn't do it on purpose. This list will help guide you to where you want to go subconsciously.

Prioritizing Engagement and Fun

By now, I think it is safe to presume that I have reiterated the importance of the feel-good chemicals that your brain releases. The easiest way to promote the release of these chemicals is through fun activities and engaging with the people around you that make you feel good.

These feel-good chemicals are what will help you to power through your workday. You will be able to focus on your work and retain and process information a lot better when your brain has the necessary amount of feel-good chemicals in the required areas. Keeping that in mind, it is important to remember that although fun and engagement might be a higher priority for those of us with ADHD, that does not mean that we should only focus on this.

It is especially easy for us to procrastinate important tasks, as well as get sidetracked by a meaningless hyperfixation or rabbit hole. As much as we try to ensure our focus remains on the important things, we're just not wired in that way. The small guilty pleasures and seemingly unimportant things are the ones that actually capture our attention.

Another aspect that we need to consider is that our hyperactivity is the main aspect of ADHD that leads to us getting distracted and being unable to focus on one thing for an extended period of time. This is why physical exercise and movement is a good thing for those of us with ADHD. When we expel our excess energy, it allows us to balance our energy levels. In essence, we focus better when we are tired.

This means that we should try to burn some energy a short time before we need to focus. Something like going for a jog in the mornings before work, doing a workout during lunchtime, or having other forms of physical activity spread out during your day will help you to be rid of enough excess energy during the day to allow you to focus better.

Physical exercise does not need to be actual exercise. Any form of movement that helps you to burn energy can be beneficial. There are many people that have opted for using standing desks while working the entire day. This keeps them from becoming too comfortable and forces them to use more energy than they would have burned while sitting and doing the exact same task.

Ideally, the activity used to balance your energy levels would be one that also releases chemicals such as dopamine. This would mean that you are able to successfully nurture the parts of your brain that would otherwise lack these chemicals, while also balancing your energy levels. This is, however, not always possible. Remember that we are each unique individuals, so although I can advise you on what the best way of dealing with ADHD is, it is up to you to decide how to implement this advice.

Finding the Right Fit

Finding the perfect job is almost as hard as finding your

soulmate. Some of us are lucky and figure it out before we even finish school. Others go their whole life without finding the special something or someone. And for some of us, we find the perfect fit, but as life happens and we change and grow, suddenly that perfect fit is no longer a fit anymore.

The point I'm trying to make here is that it is possible to find the perfect job, but doing so is extremely difficult. The best we can do is educate ourselves, learn what to look for, and see where we have the best chances for success. Luckily for us, there have been enough people with ADHD before us, so we already have some guidelines to look into.

Fast-Paced Careers

I mentioned fast-paced careers earlier as these are the most ideal career paths for someone with ADHD due to the ever-changing focus of the career. Before you become bored with the object you are focusing on, you will be focusing on something else. This also tends to mean that you would be moving around a lot more and burning more energy to help keep your hyperactivity in check. A perfect balance if your passion lies here as well.

Structured Careers

For some, the best way to deal with your ADHD is to have a rigid schedule and routine—having your day planned out to the minute while knowing what to expect and when. At the same time, when a task is completed—especially on time and on schedule—you may get the same dopamine rush that others would from having a break away from work and having a bit of fun.

The careers under this category you could look into include

- Bookkeeping/accounting

- Project management

- Factory employments

- Administrative careers

- Engineering

- Data analytics

Creative Careers

Another aspect in which people with ADHD tend to make a success for themselves is creativity. When you are unrestricted or at least less restricted by deadlines and schedules, and you can create something you feel proud of and see it grow and evolve before your eyes, you might find yourself feeling fulfilled enough to do it as a career. This is because a creative career allows you a lot more time to take breaks and recharge your focus than a traditional career would.

The careers under this category you could look into include

- Art

- Music

- Carpentry

- Construction

- Dancing

- Design

- Writing

- Beautician

- Invention

- Marketing and advertising

Passionate Careers

We've covered how important your passions in life can be, and although you might be able to find your passion in any area, there are a few career options that tend to require your passion in the first place. These can be great options for people with ADHD as it means that you will feel like you are helping someone and making a difference.

The careers under this category you could look into are

- Education

- Social work

- Healthcare

- Religious employment

Asking For Help

We still find it difficult to ask for help. This simple action feels like a major vulnerability for us. Not just as men, but as a person raised to be self-sufficient and independent. We question whether it is the right thing to do and whether it means that we can succeed as adults on our own. The answer is that, sometimes, asking for help is how someone succeeds. By knowing how and whom to ask for help, you are showing that you are an adult that can think logically and clearly. So, where do we ask for help?

Finding a Job

The first aspect we need to look at is how we find a job. Above, you learned to look for and were given examples of career paths, which is great if you already know yourself and your own interests. But this is not always the case, and it is in this aspect that it is a good idea to ask for help.

There are a number of career aptitude tests available online, and although they are a good start, I would suggest seeking out a professional to assist you in taking one. This could be your therapist or a recruitment agency. A career aptitude test is a very good way to use logical deduction to determine where you would most likely fit in and succeed.

However, for someone with ADHD, simply fitting in and succeeding does not necessarily mean that you will feel fulfilled and happy in your career, which as we know is quite important to us. This brings us to another aspect in which you could ask for assistance. Those around you tend to notice small things you don't always notice. Sitting down with your friends and family and asking them what career they could actually envision you in can be quite helpful. At the very least, it will allow you to rule out some careers that definitely do not appeal to you. Ideally, however, they will have noticed something such as you having an affinity for children or being especially good in a school subject without realizing it, that you could use to choose your career.

There is also the idea of recruitment agencies, temp agencies, or even local community centers. All three of these institutes offer a great way to be exposed to and experience different careers. Remember, taking your time to find the right fit is not failing—

it is good preparation.

It also helps to create a personal portfolio on paper. Think of it as placing your entire professional persona on the pages so that you can more easily identify the factors that will determine your success in a career. Here are some factors to consider during your job search.

Skills

Hopefully, your interests and skills go hand-in-hand. Skills include accomplishments that can reveal your competence in various work settings. Skills are often categorized this way: working with data, people, and things. I think it's safe to say that we all do best when our skills are a match for the job. What are your skills in? Data, people, or things? You can take standardized tests if you need some help identifying what you excel at. A career counselor may provide you with a skill-word list that can also help you to identify skills you may not have realized you had, may not have considered important, or hadn't considered at all.

Here is one way to reveal your interests and skills. Ask yourself these questions:

- What subjects were you best at in school?

- What would others say are your biggest strengths?

- What skills have you used to achieve your successes thus far?

- What would your teachers say your biggest strengths are?

- What do you do in your current job that makes you stand out?

Personality

What type of personality do you have? This might seem like a difficult question; "I have my own personality!" you may say. In fact, there are systematic ways to measure personality. Many organizations look for a "cultural fit" that depends on personality. You can take these tests yourself. Knowing your personality type can help you improve at work and increase your career options by letting you be not only more practical and realistic but also more confident.

Values

Everyone holds and acts on their own individual values. I think it goes without saying that we work harder when our work aligns with our values. What we value in terms of leisure time is important, too, since we want our work to also facilitate the enjoyment of our time off. None of us want to work at an organization that goes against our values. As long as your values and activities align, you will be happier and less stressed.

Aptitudes

An aptitude means you are able to easily acquire skills in a certain area, such as verbal, numerical, abstract reasoning, clerical speed, spelling, and so on. Some of these aptitudes seem straightforward, but they are actually learned. It's hard to quantify your aptitudes, but they do shine through in the working world. To put it another way, an aptitude is the ability to acquire a skill based on previous talents or abilities. You can consult a professional, such as a career counselor, about aptitudes or take a standardized test to discover them yourself. You can consult the *Dictionary of Occupational Titles* and the *Occupational Outlook Handbook* for more information.

Energy

All jobs require you to do different things. Sometimes, a job posting will come with a disclaimer saying you have to be able to stand for an extended period of time or lift a certain amount of pounds. However, some energy is metaphysical: Certain jobs are intellectually intensive, and others are physically so. Some people are "spent" after a day working retail, for instance, while others are energized by it. Try to tailor your job search and responsibilities to what you are able to and want to accomplish.

Previous Jobs

A complete history of all previous jobs that you have worked on before—even if you don't recognize them as "jobs"—can be hugely beneficial to put together. Perhaps, you helped your parents organize their paperwork when it was tax season, or you regularly babysat for the neighbors. Maybe, you helped a friend build a treehouse that one summer. These may not be seen as a career or job, but when you look at them on paper, they are quite close to what actual careers look like. So, any major task that you have taken on, even before leaving school, can be seen as a previous job and used to inform your future career choices.

At the same time, you can look at your extracurricular activities in school. Did you partake in the school newspaper? Were you a part of a planning committee? What sports did you play, or did you do band or drama?

Lastly, any place where you conducted a service in exchange for monetary compensation is indeed a job, by definition. So, even waiting tables, mowing the neighbors' lawn, or any other small favors that you got paid for could become a career.

When you have made these lists, you need to ask yourself what you learned from each of them and how you started doing that "job." Sometimes, getting the job we want is a matter of recreating past successes and learning from past mistakes.

Maintaining a Career

So, when you have found your career, how do you stop your ADHD from interfering with your ability to continuously do your job? It is so easy for someone with ADHD to become bored in the same career or position after a while, and when that happens it often leads to our quality of work deteriorating.

In essence, the best way to ensure that your ADHD doesn't negatively impact your career is to ensure that it is continuously treated. Through asking for help in the form of medication and therapy, you will achieve the best results. Therapy is not something you need to be scared of or feel embarrassed about; it can and will always be your best option to ensure that you effectively adapt to any new challenges your ADHD throws your way. Your mental health practitioner will also be able to adjust your ADHD medication to ensure that you enjoy as many of the benefits as possible, with as few of the side effects.

Ideally, you would have both a therapist for your ADHD and a career counselor. I say this because there is never such a thing as too much help. Your therapist would be able to attend to your mental health and well-being, while a career counselor will be more equipped to help you face the challenges of your work life. When the two are combined, you can think of them as your success team—a group of advisors there to help you achieve success.

Before you feel bad, I want you to remember that this advice is the same for anyone, not just people with ADHD. Those that do not have ADHD could also benefit from having their own success team—theirs might just look a bit different.

CHAPTER 7

Dating With ADHD

Now that we've covered your career, we need to look into your personal life and, most importantly, your relationships.

Dating is extremely difficult, made even more difficult by modern times. We have dating apps, social distancing, sociopolitical movements, and so many other factors that are always working against us. ADHD does not have to work against this, and it can actually be a powerful ally in our battle against loneliness.

However, before we proceed, I do want to take a moment to address something I just mentioned that may have raised eyebrows: sociopolitical movements. We live in a time when men and our actions are under intense scrutiny. Women have made it very clear that they do not feel safe and comfortable when meeting with men. They go through a variety of preparations just to meet someone—such as sharing a live location with friends, sending your picture as well as the date, time, and location of the date to multiple people, and giving a check-in timeline during which time their friends need to ensure that they are, indeed, safe.

Now, although most men are not part of the problem, we do unfortunately still suffer the consequences and need to do our part to alleviate the issue. This is also one aspect where our ADHD could pose as an obstacle, especially since we tend to become bored with the same scenery very quickly, and we are impulsive and energetic enough to suggest going to another location as well—which can read as a red flag since our date will not have had time to vet this location and enact a plan of safety.

These are a few of the aspects we need to look at, and the key to a successful date is to ensure that both parties feel comfortable and happy the entire time. Platforms such as dating apps can help us a lot to ensure that someone is comfortable before meeting us, but they also pose the danger of making us lose focus.

There is something to be said for the old-fashioned and romanticized way of dating. That idea of accidentally meeting someone through the normal course of your life and getting caught up with each other. Although it sounds like a movie, this way is, indeed, still the easiest way of dating, especially for those of us with ADHD.

Creating Intentional Opportunities for Connection

There are multiple ways to create an intentional opportunity. These don't have to be restricted to either online or in person; the most important thing is to put yourself out there. So, how do we do this?

Dating Apps

Dating apps are a very good place to get started. At the very least, using dating apps will help you to get into the mindset of how to approach and engage with prospective partners, as well as what the important information is to share with them.

When using a dating app, it's easy for us to become overwhelmed by all the prospective choices. In fact, this is actually how dating apps are designed, so they can still make money. There are constantly new faces being shown to you, and before you can see the next choice, you need to decide regarding this one. Your mind starts working at 1,000 miles per minute and you find yourself making superficial and impulsive choices. This means that you'll probably remain on the app much longer than you would have if you had made a well-thought-out choice every time.

Yet, we still find that we swipe right on quite a lot of people, and when it comes to chatting to these people, you have so many conversations going on that you can't actually be mindful of what you are saying. In essence, dating apps promote shallow and superficial interactions that are designed to not go too far, otherwise the dating site would become obsolete. This tactic is especially effective against people with ADHD and can make it so much harder for us to find a partner through these apps.

Luckily, there is a solution called intentional dating. This technique was actually developed by a French dating app called *Once*, and the basic essence behind it is that it only allows you to match with one person per day.

The idea behind this is to ensure that you do not waste your swipes and matches on quantity, but that you instead focus on quality. This also forces you to ensure that you put yourself forward as a quality person and that your profile will be well put together. When you are communicating with only a handful of people—especially people that you know you have put thought and energy into matching with and who have done the same for you—you will feel more comfortable and be able to give them more of your attention and energy.

So, let's look at how to actually engage in intentional dating.

What Do You Want?

The first step is to ensure that you know exactly what you want in a partner. What attracts you to a person, what makes you want to spend more time with a person, and what pushes you away? To do this, you can make a list. Actually, you'll want to make four lists.

The four lists will be

- **What I want in a person:** This consists of things that would be very nice, but that are not deal-breakers in any way. Think of these as added perks. You could include something like someone that is a dog person or someone that enjoys activities in nature, such as camping.

- **What I need in a person:** This is essentially what this person has to bring to the table or what you require them to offer so that you can ensure you are both completely compatible. These items might be deal-breakers if they are not there, although as long as they meet most of these requirements, there is still a possible match. These could be something like a person following the same religion as you, someone that understands the challenges of mental health, or perhaps, someone that is comfortable in social situations so that they can help guide you through it.

- **What I won't put up with:** These are the hard limits—the things that tell you that you will most definitely not be compatible with the person. Perhaps, it is something that will require you to change or that infringes on your values. For example, someone that is overly religious or not religious at all, someone that does not like animals, or someone that refuses to work.

- **What I cannot go without:** These are definite deal-breakers for you. This is something you absolutely require from someone, and if even one item on this list is not met you and the person will be incompatible. Think along the lines of, the person must not be anti-smoking because you are a smoker, or they must be family-oriented because you want children.

Your lists will be created using your feelings. So although I said that *I* cannot go without someone that is family-oriented, that may not be as high of a priority for you. Remember, my examples are there as guidelines, every person's list will look wildly different from yours. I also want to stress the fact that you should not place any of these demands and requirements on your profile, unless the dating app you use specifically asks for it. Although it is important that we all know what we want, adding a checklist to your profile is generally seen as self-centered. Your checklist is something that is very personal to you and can come across as insulting when telling someone that they simply don't tick all your boxes, especially since it is very fluid and could change at any time based on your personal environment or even the influence of those around you. So, be sure that you update this private list frequently to keep it in line with your current personal preferences.

The second step to take is to make sure that you know why you are dating. Are you just dating because you don't want to be alone, or are you actually looking for a long-term partner to face the challenges of life with you? Are you just looking for temporary and short-lived company? This is a point that will be very important to place on your dating profile. In this way, you ensure that anyone who is a prospective match knows what you are there for and what to expect from you.

Remember, there is no shame in wanting whatever you want; the only shame is in not being honest about it.

Honesty and Authenticity

We've already covered the overlap between what you want and being honest about it. However, that is not where being authentic ends. When you do start engaging with someone— especially with the intent of dating them in the future—it is reasonable to want to impress them and put your best foot forward. This is great, as long as you ensure that this still represents your personality accurately.

The problem is when we suppress aspects of our true personality in order to try and get someone to like us, they don't truly like *us*. They, instead, like the character we are showing them, and eventually, as you become more comfortable with this person, it will become more and more difficult to keep playing this character. Your true personality will always break through, and the other person will start to feel like you are no longer the same person that they started dating.

This is why it is important to be yourself from the beginning. Be that person who is unapologetically themselves at all times. This will not only help you to find someone that you truly match up with, but it will also save both of you time not wasted on someone that you do not get along with. This additionally means that you will feel more comfortable and less drained after having an interaction with these people. Intimacy and trust will come more easily and feel more natural.

Remember, the best person to be is you. Nobody else can be you, as well as you can be you.

Getting Uncomfortable

You may have noticed that being uncomfortable is a recurring theme. This is so in all aspects of life, regardless of having ADHD or not. You will often need to be uncomfortable in order to get used to a situation, and dating is no different. Now, I'm not saying you need to go on dates with people that make you feel uncomfortable, but instead be cognizant that having the difficult conversations regarding who and what you are, what you are looking for, and where you're coming from is what is important. In fact, having these conversations and allowing yourself to show that you are being vulnerable to a person and a bit uncomfortable with this situation is a great way to gain respect and trust.

Us men with ADHD so regularly force ourselves to play the role we think society wants from us that being uncomfortable often means you are being your own authentic self. I also want to remind you of what I said earlier: Women, globally, are scared and mostly uncomfortable with meeting men, especially someone from a website that is technically a stranger. There is a joke that has been going around for a few years that says, "When we were kids we were told not to get into cars with strangers and not to meet strangers on the internet. Now, we ask a stranger on the internet to let us into their car so that we can go meet another stranger from the internet." For women, the discomfort that this invokes is so much worse since it makes it a lot easier for predators to gain access to them. So, if they are already so uncomfortable, I'm sure we can suffer through a bit of discomfort as well, especially if this will help make them more comfortable around us. Regardless of the gender of your potential romantic partners, it's always helpful to keep in mind that they are probably just as apprehensive as you are. New experiences are scary, but we owe it to ourselves and our dates to approach every encounter with an open mind.

Choices

Dating apps offer us so many choices. There are usually thousands of profiles just a short distance from you. When you leave the area you normally work and live in, even more profiles become available. When you leave your town or state to go visit another place, your potential matches double, if not triple. So how, in this ocean of possibilities, do we make the correct choice?

Usually, there are a few points that stand as an obstacle to our choices. These points tend to force us into making poor decisions when it comes to our dating, and once we understand them, we know how to avoid them:

- **Being unsure about love:** We live in a society where we can much more easily share our experiences with each other. As humans, there is something within us that just makes negative experiences seem so much more interesting. Perhaps, it is because we love to envision ourselves in that experience and imagine how we would have handled it better, or perhaps, it is because we like hearing that someone has it worse than we do so that we can feel better about our own life. Regardless, we are always hearing about something negative. This includes divorces, break-ups, and other relationship horror stories. Eventually, we hear so many negatives about relationships, and we ourselves have negative relationship experiences, that the next thing we know, we find ourselves wondering if love truly exists.

- **We're not sure what a healthy relationship truly is:** This is another result of our environment. We are bombarded with so many images of what a relationship is supposed to look like that we are not always sure which are healthy and which are not. I want you to think back to the most popular shows in the late 80s and early 90s. These are shows that, for many people my age, formed our opinions. Yet, when we look back at them now, we realize that the relationships in these shows were definitely not healthy. Despite this, they have been—and to a point *still* get—romanticized. This means that when we enter a relationship, we often strive to be like these unhealthy relationships, and this leads us to make unhealthy decisions.

- **We have a poor self-image:** When we don't hold ourselves in high regard, we tend to overestimate our own limits. When we feel this way, we may find ourselves attracted to someone that often shares this point of view, instead of someone that builds us up because we think those that think less of us are more honest.

- **We're scared of being alone:** Very often we'll date not because we are ready for a long-term relationship or because we actually want to make a commitment to someone, but rather, simply because we don't want to go home to an empty place. We want another voice in the house just to make us feel less cut off from the world. This often leads us to a commitment with someone we are not really compatible with—someone we don't really want to spend the rest of our lives with.

When we see the signs that we are dating for one of the above reasons, we need to understand that it is not a good idea to continue the relationship. In the end, we are only hurting ourselves and others.

How Do I Implement Intentional Dating?

Now that we understand what intentional dating is, how do we implement it in our daily dating activities?

I'll preface this by saying the key to intentional dating is to continuously reassess yourself and any situation pertaining to your dating. This means that you should be reassessing your dating profile, your acceptance criteria, your goals, your intentions, and your actions. It is easy to say that every month, on the first of the month, you will open your dating profile, update the oldest picture, and reassess your biography. The rest, however, is a bit hard to schedule. So, the best way to do this is to assess every interaction you had and see what events during this date or conversation felt off or wrong for you.

Then, lastly, the best way to implement intentional dating from the get-go is by ensuring that every day, you only match with one person. Try to only swipe right or attempt to match with 10 profiles, and ensure that you read through each and every profile before you make a decision.

By doing this and ensuring that you follow all the other

guidelines I've set out for you, dating apps will start to show a lot more meaningful matches.

Traditional Dating

There are a large number of people that have decided to return to the old ways of dating. They have done this because dating apps have become notorious for being a place to find meaningless sex or a free meal. So now, instead, they are once again taking steps to meet people in real life and form a meaningful connection from there.

This comes with its own wave of challenges but is often more suitable for someone with ADHD since it is not designed to play on your short attention span. The benefits also spread a lot further than just not being targeted by a company for your money. You also eliminate most of the dangers and pressures of online dating.

By meeting someone in person, the immediate pressure to prove that you are "marriage material" is eliminated, along with the assumption that you are meeting purely for romantic purposes. This also allows you to be yourself, you don't necessarily have to impress someone, and you don't feel like you are constantly being watched and graded on your behavior. It is also easier to get to know someone while engaged in an activity that most likely aligns with mutual interests than it would be while just sitting down for a cup of coffee.

Before we get into the rules of offline dating, let's look at how and where you can meet someone away from the internet:

- Events for singles

- Networking events through your career

- High school or college reunions

- Sports clubs and groups

- Gyms

- Via friends—whether through being set up or at a social gathering

- Hobbies

- Religious activities—church, bake sales, outreach projects, etc.

- Volunteer groups

- Activity groups—book clubs, camping or hiking groups, etc.

- Cafes, bars, or clubs

- Dog parks

Essentially, any place where a group of people with similar

interests get together is a good place for you to meet someone. There is, however, a very important set of rules that you need to understand and follow. Especially when it comes to women, people might feel uncomfortable when being approached out of the blue. This is particularly true when they are engaging in an activity on their own. Try to keep the following in mind:

- **They might not want you to talk to them at all:** You can do everything right—you can be respectful, charming, decent, and every other positive thing you can think of—but the fact remains that sometimes people just don't want to be approached by a man they don't know. This doesn't mean that you shouldn't try to approach people at all. But perhaps, look at what they are doing before deciding whether to approach. If they have earphones in or are clearly engaged in an activity, it is probably best not to bother them. If you think it is safe to approach a person, by all means, do so. Just be prepared to acknowledge that you might be rejected from the start.

- **Look at the situation:** I've mentioned it quite a bit at the start of the chapter, but remember that others, but especially women, are often unsure about the true intentions of a man. Almost every woman has a story of a man overreacting to being rejected—sometimes to the point of violence. This means that when a woman is alone with a man, especially if in a confined space, she is already alert and on edge. The same goes if she is approached by a group of men. She has no way to know that you are not a danger to her and that you mean her no harm. So, be sure never to approach anyone unless you are both in a very public space where they can feel safe. Even then, starting your conversation with something along the lines of "I'm sorry to bother you…" can go a long way to making them feel more comfortable.

- **Watch what you say:** Men, in general, prefer to communicate a lot more directly. Women's communication, on the other hand, can be complex to the point that we often have trouble understanding them. However, these are both only generalizations, and everyone has their own preferred method of communication. As a result, it is best to err on the side of caution by being as open and welcoming of a conversation partner as possible. So, instead of approaching and saying, "Hi, you're hot. Can I have your number?" try starting an actual conversation. In this way, you get a chance to measure whether or not the person is interested in you, and they tend to feel more comfortable. If the conversation is good, they will want to continue it and will be a lot more comfortable sharing their number or taking yours than they would when they have never spoken to you before. You can start a conversation about literally anything and, yes, that includes talking about the weather.

- **When and what to compliment:** Generally speaking,

starting a conversation with someone by complimenting their body makes them feel uncomfortable, objectified, and quite certain that your intentions are nothing more than sexual. If you do, however, feel that you would like to start with a compliment, the best way is to use your ADHD to your advantage. You may notice something unconventional that others don't, and you can compliment them on that. Remember that complimenting clothing means that you've looked at their body, so that can feel like you might be sexualizing them. But saying something like, "Your hair looks amazing," or "Your dog is adorable, and the bond between you two seems very special," can get you a lot further.

- **What their body language says:** This is especially difficult for people with ADHD. You don't always pick up on the body language of a specific person because that means that you need to focus on them. Luckily, there are a few obvious ways to determine when someone is uncomfortable. If you do determine that they are uncomfortable, the best thing to do is to leave them alone. This is often enough for the person to see that you mean no harm and that you do, indeed, respect them and their boundaries, and who knows, this might be the reason they approach you for further conversation later on. When someone crosses their arms or places their bag or some other object between the two of you, they are uncomfortable. Similarly, if they do not make eye contact or only briefly make eye contact, they are uncomfortable. They might also give you short answers without asking any questions back or make up an excuse to put some distance between the two of you. If you see any of these signs, they are not interested in you.

- **The ball is in their court:** Let's say you approached a person, struck up a conversation, and they were nice throughout. They engaged, interacted, and really seemed interested. Now that you've reached the end of the conversation, how do you get their number? Well, you don't. You've made the first move and opened up a dialogue, but they still need to be the one to decide whether or not they would like to continue it. Offering to provide your own number rather than asking a person for theirs is usually perceived much more positively. A simple "Here's my number, I would really like to continue talking to you," leaves the choice of continuing the conversation in their hands, while letting them know that you are interested.

I realize that these rules for approaching others sound tedious and hard. But believe me when I say that your chances of approaching a prospective partner will be greatly improved if you follow them. People want nothing more than to be respected and treated well, and these are the guidelines they have given us, which means that these are the roadmap to success.

Other than that, the same rules of honesty and authenticity apply to any interaction you have with your prospective partner. This is, luckily, a much easier task to accomplish when you meet someone as yourself in the first place. It is, however, a lot more difficult of a situation to walk away from.

In the end, both traditional dating and online dating have their own set of challenges and benefits. There is nothing to keep you from trying out both techniques. The only way to find out which way works best for you, regardless of ADHD, is by plunging in headfirst and finding out.

Be Proactive

ADHD means that you will very easily get distracted. When you are distracted, you can very easily neglect those around you. This includes your partner. With ADHD, it is quite easy to not even realize that you are distracted and that you are neglecting those around you.

At first, you think you're just answering a text message, then you are just watching a video on *Facebook*, and the next thing you know you are glued to your phone while your partner is next to you on the couch, feeling like your phone is a wall between the two of you.

This, of course, does not only apply to your phone. In the hands of a person with ADHD, anything can be a distraction. This is why we need to be proactive. We need to take extra steps to ensure that we spend time with our partners. The best way to do so is to get rid of all your distractions during times in which you want to ensure that you spend time with your partner. It is also important that you ensure you schedule time with your partner. Even if you just invite them to come spend time at your home, leave your phone in the kitchen, put away your gaming console remotes, and keep the television off if you can.

The same rules apply if you are going out with your partner. Make sure that you keep yourself and your area distraction-free for the duration of your date.

ADHD, however, means that distraction is not the only challenge we face. I've explained the challenges we face with our emotions earlier in the book. Add that to being a man—shouldering all that is expected of us under the label of "masculinity"—and you have someone that has great difficulty with understanding and expressing their emotions. This means that you have yet another aspect of your relationship in which you have to be proactive. This is a bit more difficult than scheduling time with your partner and hiding away your distractions. You cannot schedule your displays of affection; you cannot schedule showing your emotions. In doing so, they would no longer be genuine.

The best way to ensure that you show your emotions is to

remind yourself continuously that they do exist. This can be done by adding this relationship to your affirmations every morning or by ensuring that you have reminders during the day that are not timed or superficial. A major challenge that we face with ADHD is that when we do not have a constant reminder, our distractions and hyperfixations take over almost the entirety of our minds. The idea of "out of sight, out of mind" is more applicable to people with ADHD due to this fact.

In essence, when we don't have a constant reminder of someone or something, our mind is filled with so many other things that we completely forget that that person or thing even exists. So, having a constant reminder of our partner—something like a picture of their face as your wallpaper or a photograph of them on your desk—that will be in your general view can bring them back into your mind at irregular intervals. Then, each and every time you see this reminder of them, make sure that you let them know that you are, indeed, thinking of them.

ADHD forces us to be proactive toward various aspects of our lives. This is not always easy, especially when it comes to dating. The mistakes everyone else makes in relationships are amplified within us. We find it a lot more difficult to actually engage with our partners and to remain focused on them. This is exactly the reason why we need to work so much harder to ensure that our partners receive the attention and affection that they require.

Just Say It

One of the largest obstacles we place in front of ourselves is how to tell our prospective partners that we have ADHD. So often, we wonder whether they will look at us differently, whether they will start to blame all of the problems in the relationship on our diagnosis, and whether they will be prepared to stay with us through all our obstacles.

The good news is that, as far as mental health diagnoses go, ADHD is a very accepted and relatively mild diagnosis. The bad news is that people tend to feel so due to the fact that they do not understand ADHD very well and are under the impression that it is a diagnosis that only affects children. This also means that there is a very good possibility that some people may not understand or even accept that you do, in fact, have an ADHD diagnosis.

The truth, however, is that you will never know how your prospective partner will react to the diagnosis unless you tell them directly. With online dating, it is a lot easier. You can put this bit of information in your profile and hope that everyone you match with does actually read your profile in its entirety.

With someone you meet offline, it is a bit more difficult. We don't walk around with a dating profile we can just hand out to every new person we meet. This means that you will need to find the correct time to tell someone. The correct time to bring it up.

The first date is often seen as the most important interaction up until an engagement. This is because the first date is the time when you are supposed to share about yourself and decide whether or not you want to pursue a relationship with each other. This also means that it is the perfect time to bring up your diagnosis.

Be direct about it, and be honest about it. The best way to share any information is to rip the band-aid off and just say it.

Make Notes of the Important Things

Another way to ensure that you are successful in your dating ventures is to ensure that you remember the important things about your partner. This is extremely difficult for the simple reason that as soon as you hear about them, you fixate on it; you will be interested and will believe that you will remember this small bit of information about them. However, as soon as some new information pops into your mind, that important aspect will be gone forever.

This is why it is important to make notes of these little tidbits of information—preferably as soon as you receive them. Of course, it might seem a bit creepy to be writing down every bit of information about your partner. There are more stealthy ways in which you can do it. The best ways are to send yourself some texts or to repeat the information in your mind until you are alone and can write it down.

I want you to think about how your partner would feel if in a year, or even 10 years, you bring up a random fact about them that they did not think was important, but that you did. This would not only show that you were listening but also provide a demonstration of how much you care about them and truly *know* them. This is why it is important to write down the important things that you learn about your partner. It is a way of showing affection and reassuring them that they are actually a priority for you.

Monitor Your Urge to Be Impulsive

The next aspect of ADHD that tends to complicate our relationships is our impulsivity. We don't always realize when we are impulsive, and it is difficult to refrain from acting on these impulses.

When we do act on these impulses, it usually leads to us neglecting our partner. This makes monitoring and controlling these urges so much more important. There is a time and place for us to be impulsive, and even a time when it could be appropriate—or even romantic—to act on these impulses. The deciding factor here is the involvement of your partner.

When you have been honest with your partner regarding your ADHD, it also means that you can be honest about your symptoms and side effects. We'll cover communication skills more in-depth in just a moment, but for now, the important thing is to ensure that you do communicate these feelings and take those of your partner into account.

When you feel the urge to be impulsive and to do something in the spur of the moment, the first thing you need to ask yourself is whether or not this action will impact either you or your partner in any negative way. Assess the ripple effect your impulse will have, and if you determine that it will cause waves, ensure that you do whatever it takes to refrain from this impulse.

If you believe that this impulse has acceptable risks and that acting upon it will not affect you or your partner negatively, then your next step should be to contact your partner—especially if you had plans with them. Talk to your partner, and share your possible impulse with them. Go another step further, and ask them if they would like to join you on your impulse.

By sharing your impulse with your partner, you are not only showing them that they do matter to you, and that you are considering their emotions, but also attempting to make them a part of your world.

There is a downside to all of this, however. If you are constantly acting on your impulses, your partner might start to think that you are unreliable and that you have absolutely no impulse control. This is why it is so important that you need to monitor and control these urges.

Treatments, like therapy and medication, will help you to have the impulses less often and to be more resistant towards these urges.

Hone Your Communication Skills

Communication tends to be a bigger problem for men, than for people with ADHD as a whole. However, this does not change the fact that ADHD also does have an impact on your communication skills. The irony in the situation is that communication can help you to more easily manage your ADHD. And of course, when it comes to a relationship, communication is key. This means that you have multiple reasons to hone your communication skills. This set of skills is comprised of the following:

- **Listening:** The people around you, especially your partner, want to know that you are listening to them. You need to pay attention to what they tell you, and focus on taking in the information instead of on how you want to respond to them. They need to feel like they are the most important person in the world while having a conversation with you. When they say something you are not sure of, don't be afraid of asking them to clarify for you. Your ADHD also means that you will be more inclined to try and multitask multiple conversations. While someone is sitting in front of you talking to you, you might try to respond to an email or text message. This could make the person you are talking to feel as if you are not interested in their conversation. Try to remain a wholly active participant in the conversation.

- **Remember who you are talking to:** We communicate differently with different people. When you are talking to your friends, you might be more relaxed with your tone of voice, you might not be too worried about how your words are perceived. When you are talking to someone in a professional capacity, you will try to remove all tone and emotion from your words and just try to get information across or, perhaps, exaggerate politeness to encourage collaboration in the workplace. So, what should your tone look like with your partner? If you treat them like your friends, they could feel like you do not care about hurting their feelings. If you treat them like a coworker, they might feel like you have no feelings towards them or are simply trying to placate them. The best way to talk to your partner is to be truly comfortable but still approach them with reverence and respect. You want to ensure that they understand their opinions are valued above the opinions of others and also that you feel comfortable enough to discuss any topic with them.

- **Body language speaks:** Remember that your body might say things that your mouth refuses to. It is only natural to turn your body towards whatever your true focus is or to cross your arms when you feel insecure or even attacked. These subtle cues will tell your partner where your mind is and what your feelings are. So, be sure that your mouth and body communicate the same thing and that you do not send out mixed signals.

- **Check your messages:** Especially when you are communicating with your partner, you want to make sure that they feel like you have put effort into your messages to them. When they receive a message from you filled with spelling mistakes and poor sentence construction, they might feel like your attention was elsewhere when you were supposed to be responding to them or that you rushed it because you have something more important than answering them that you would much rather get to. Make sure that even text messages show your partner how much you care about them.

- **Don't be afraid to call:** When you want to discuss something important or you feel like your tone is being misunderstood over a text message, don't be afraid to pick up your phone and call your partner. A phone call is a lot more personal than a text message, and it shows that you are willing to take time out of your day to have an uninterrupted conversation with them.

- **Think about it before you say it:** Being impulsive means that you tend to blurt out something before you have thought about whether it is a good idea to say it. It is with great difficulty that you will eventually teach yourself to think about what you are about to say, before you blurt it out. But the more you force yourself to practice this habit, the more you will learn it, and the less embarrassment and arguments it will cause.

- **Smile:** It's been proven that just by faking a smile, you can even improve your own mood. Aside from that, a smile can be calming and help you to let your partner feel more comfortable in a conversation with you. Plus, your partner will usually enjoy seeing you happy, as this often means they are making you happy which boosts their confidence.

Ask for Support

We've discussed asking for help and support before. By now, I hope that I have reiterated the fact that you do not need to feel ashamed to ask someone to help or support you. That being said, I understand that, at times, it is easier to ask for support from a total stranger than it is to ask someone you know, especially someone you feel you should be helping and supporting yourself. To this end, I would like to share some advice with you on how to ask your partner or spouse for support.

First, I would like to clarify that asking your partner for support might not necessarily mean requesting assistance financially or physically, it could be emotional support or even mental support. Whichever type of support you are asking for, it is definitely okay to ask your partner, that is what they are there for, and mutual support is a foundational element of being in a relationship.

What Support Do You Need?

The first step is to ask yourself what support you need. What do you require from your partner? Especially when you need emotional support, it is helpful to sit down and write out what you need, how you would like to feel, and what actions they could take to help you achieve these feelings. Then, add to that, and write down why you need it or why this form of support is so important to you. By the end of this exercise, you should have a very clear idea of exactly what you want, and how to explain it clearly and purposefully to your partner.

What Do You Want Your Partner to Think?

This is perhaps the most important question. When you ask your partner for assistance, you need to think about what they are going to think. When they tell themselves why you asked for their assistance, what reasoning will they give themselves? This will be directly informed by how you approach them and how you formulate your communication. So, do you want them to think you are asking for their support because you need them and trust them, because you have no other choice, or just because they are better equipped at handling the situation? All three of these examples could be correct under different circumstances, so you will need to determine which circumstance requires which reaction and prepare yourself to deliver the correct message.

How Do You Raise the Issue?

When you approach your partner with a serious issue, it will feel natural to sound and appear serious as well. Unfortunately, this can cause your partner to enter what I refer to as "professional mode." I see all of us as having two dominant personalities: The one is our work personality, used when we are in professional mode—our answers are guarded, our mind is working in a little box that revolves around cost-to-company, available resources, schedules, deadlines, timelines, etc. The other is our "offline mode." This is our personality when we are with friends and family, and it revolves around our emotions. We don't need to be too logical, but we can instead focus on whether this will create a positive memory and strengthen bonds. Unfortunately, when someone approaches us in a serious way, our professional mode tends to kick in because we prepare for crisis management and damage control. For many of us, this is something that happens in our work life on a daily basis, so our professional mode is more equipped to deal with this situation.

This is why it is of the utmost importance to keep your partner relaxed and offline. You don't want them to shut off their emotions, especially not if you require emotional support. So, when approaching them, use a soft and melodic voice. This will comfort and reassure them and keep them in their partner headspace. Also, make sure not to push them into anything by saying something along the lines of, "Honey, you've been very distant from me for far too long, it's time we talk about it." This will make them feel pressured and is a sure way of activating their professional mode. Instead, try saying something like, "Hey honey, I'm a bit concerned because I've been feeling that we're not as close as we used to be anymore. I would really like your input on this, can we talk about it when you're up for it please?" In the second example, you told them what is going on, but you also made it clear that you don't want them to feel uncomfortable or pressured, and you are still taking their feelings into account.

Body Language Speaks, Again

We've covered this before, so I won't go into too much detail again. But I do, however, want you to remember that your body language could give away some thoughts you don't want to make known. With this in mind, be sure that you pay attention to your eye contact, tone of voice, what you are doing with your hands and arms, etc.

Especially when you are asking for support from your partner, you cannot be facing away from them, staring into your lap while picking at your fingers. This could let your partner feel that you are ashamed of asking them for help, which means that you do not trust them completely. You also shouldn't get too worked up, as this may make them feel that they are somehow to blame for what is bothering you. Always try to remain as calm and open as possible.

Boundaries

Boundaries are very hard to set up and even more difficult to follow. The boundaries—and the consequences for overstepping these boundaries—will vary in each situation. These boundaries should also apply to both parties and be created together. Remember that if you create boundaries for another person and try to force them to follow these boundaries, they become rules instead. The healthiest boundaries set up in a relationship are those that have been placed together through compromises.

If you require financial support from a partner and promise to pay them back monthly, that is an agreement. The boundaries you set in place will, for example, be that you cannot continue living above your financial means until they are paid back in full, and should you overstep these boundaries, you are expected to pay them back in full immediately. However, a boundary for your partner would be that they are not allowed to question your financial situation as long as you keep up payments, and if they overstep, the consequence would be that they should start paying for joined activities.

When the support required is emotional, your boundaries will again seem a bit different. These could be things such as that for the first hour you see each other for the day, neither is allowed to even touch their phone, unless there is a phone call regarding an emergency. The consequence for overstepping this boundary could be something along the lines of the guilty party having to take the other one on a romantic evening out. This is a fun way to enforce boundaries while still building the relationship. You just need to ensure that your boundaries are always fair and productive.

Check-Ins

When you are asking your partner to support you in any way, you are asking them to divert some of their own resources your way. When I say "resources," I mean mental and physical energy, time, money, or even just emotions. Whatever you need

106

them to give you extra of will mean that they take it away from somewhere else. If you need them to show you more affection, they will take mental energy away from their daily work to think of ways to show affection; they will take time out of their day to make an effort for you; and they will use more emotional time that they could have spent processing their own day to instead share that emotional availability with you. It is for this reason that you need to check in with them regularly. Make sure that supporting you is not causing them to make mistakes or neglect other parts of their life. While checking in, you can also share whether or not you are receiving the support you need, and even thank them. You can also share the progress you have made due to their support.

Thank Them

Their support does not just extend to what you have asked them to help with. A partner will often do little things like make you coffee in the morning, have lunch delivered during the day, or just take you out for a drink after a rough day, without being asked. Recognize the small things they do to try and help out of love—above and beyond the support you asked for—and make sure to thank them for it. Even if it's not something you actually need or want from them, they took some of their resources and gave them to you because they care, and it helps to make sure they know that you do appreciate it.

Take Emotional Responsibility

When we have a partner, we often rely on them to calm us down during times of distress. We rely on them to make our home environment or social situations pleasant and fun. We rely on them to make us feel happy. This has become so normal and romanticized that we don't even think about it twice. The fact is that if you are relying on someone else for your emotions, you are not in a healthy relationship.

If you are someone that relies on another person for emotional stability and gratification, I don't want you to feel ashamed about it. This happens to all of us at some point, and there are many factors that contribute to why we are doing this. The key is to realize it and to work on yourself to change this. When you start taking emotional responsibility, the health of your relationship will start to improve, any connections you have with other people will become stronger, and your mood overall will improve.

So, how do we take responsibility for our own emotions?

You Cannot Change People

Have you ever had a partner that made a room feel like it went ten shades darker as soon as they entered it? Look at what your feelings were in that moment. Were you feeling guilt or responsibility? Understand that if someone enters a room already in a negative headspace before you've even had an interaction with them, that is not your fault, and you should not be the one responsible for changing those emotions. The first step to taking responsibility for your own emotions is by letting go of the responsibility for the emotions of others.

This does not just apply to your partner coming home in a foul mood. Any emotion your partner or anyone else around you feels is their own responsibility. When they get mad at a waiter for getting their order wrong, or they become frustrated in traffic, that is all on them, not on you.

I, I, I

The way we think and speak is a lot more powerful than we realize. By changing a single word in a sentence, you can change the entire meaning of that sentence. For example, if I had instead said "by changing a single word in a sentence, you can *fix* the entire meaning of that sentence." I would have implied that the sentence was incorrect to start with, but by saying "change," I imply that the sentence was correct, but could have more than one meaning.

The word I want you to start using in your sentences more, is "I." Instead of telling your partner, "you make me sad when you are late," try saying, "I feel sad when you're late." In this way, you are taking responsibility for your own emotions. The reason we do this is that when we tell our partner that they made us sad by being late, we are transferring guilt onto them, so even if they were late because of an accident on the road that caused traffic, we are still making it their problem. Whereas if we just share what emotion we experience, they don't have that sense of guilt and will be far more likely to feel empathy.

Don't Assume They Know What You Want

If you have a need or an emotional reaction that you wish to avoid, don't expect your partner to just figure it out. Tell them exactly what you need, and communicate openly and honestly. I want you to think about your partner being on a trip with friends. They will probably be doing some fun activities and enjoying the distractions that such trips are meant for. Although you might worry about them being far away, they don't share your perspective and won't necessarily think of anticipating your needs. This is why you need to tell them what your needs are. For example, "I tend to worry a lot when I know you are traveling. Could I please ask you to let me know when you arrive at your destination safely, and just check in to say that you are okay once in a while?"

By doing this, you show them that you care about them, and you are not making them responsible for your emotions. You are, instead, asking them for support.

Take Heed of Your Own Actions

We've already established that we cannot change those around us, but we can change ourselves. If your partner does something that makes you feel unhappy, you have a choice on how to react. You can confront them about their actions—and, in turn, make yourself even more upset by arguing—or you can choose to rather find a solution to the problem that might be beneficial to both of you.

If your partner regularly forgets to put gas in their car, you will naturally become upset if you have to take them gas every couple of days. Instead of lecturing them about remembering to check their gas every day, you can send them a text message in the mornings around the time they leave for work and ask them if they have enough gas in the car or tell them every time you refill your car and ask if they also need to refill. This not only helps you to keep your emotions in a more positive place but also helps to reassure your partner that you do care about them.

Question Your Thoughts

Earlier in the book, we spoke about how we tend to think, and how to change our thoughts to a more positive narrative. The same applies here, just to a different set of thoughts.

As humans, we will make mistakes. Those around us will make mistakes. None of us are perfect. It is only natural for us to react negatively toward a mistake that affects us. So although we can determine, through our choices, how much it affects us, our involuntary responses also have an impact on us. If your partner drops a glass for example, you may choose not to react negatively and simply help them clean up and move on, which is great. Yet, in your mind, you might be thinking "This is why I can't have nice stuff. Somebody is always dropping stuff and breaking my things." These types of thoughts could prolong the negative feelings we experience, even when we decide not to act on them.

To combat this, you should question it. When a thought like this pops into your mind, ask yourself whether that thought is truly accurate or not. Are you not just, perhaps, judging out of anger? Most often, the answer is that these thoughts are born from anger and overestimating the seriousness of the situation—as for the other times, buy metal glasses, they don't break so easily.

Take Responsibility for the Emotions You Cause

Although the everyday emotions of others are not your responsibility, there are emotions you can cause through your actions. If we take the glass example from above, and say that your reaction was instead to yell at your partner and tell them they did something wrong, you are responsible for the feelings of guilt and sadness they will inevitably have, even though it was an accident. When something like this happens, take a second, breathe, and immediately apologize to them. Express your regret for allowing yourself to be taken over by your negative emotions. Explain to them that your emotions were not because *they* broke a glass, but instead that a glass had broken, and that you do not blame them for something that happens accidentally. Explain that they were not responsible for your emotions. In this way, you are taking responsibility for your own actions and emotions. Just make sure that you do not make excuses or stray from the current circumstances—such as by saying you got mad because four of your glasses had broken that week alone. This is not taking responsibility but instead deflecting responsibility to whoever broke the other four glasses.

Self-Care

Holding others responsible for our emotional well-being can often be a result of us not finding a way to ensure it for ourselves. This can be due to life just being too busy, depression, or even just our ADHD making it extremely difficult. The best way to combat this is to make sure that we find a way of de-stressing and processing our emotions. Self-care is the best way to do so. Self-care can be something as basic as just improving our diet, sitting in the garden for a few hours, or any other action that brings us joy and helps us to process all these emotions.

Get Away From Negative People

We've already established that we need to stop holding ourselves responsible for the emotional well-being of others. At the same time, we need to ensure that when others make us feel negative emotions, we don't allow these emotions to fester and grow. But what happens when we have somebody in our life who is constantly causing negative emotions within us and trying to force responsibility for their emotions on us?

There comes a point where you need to identify that just having someone in your life is causing you to feel consistently negative. These people are actively harmful to your emotional well-being. And although yes, they are the cause, by keeping them in your life you are allowing them to make you feel negative. You are still responsible for those negative emotions because you are the one letting them in. In order to combat this, take responsibility, and get rid of these negative emotions, you may need to control your exposure to the cause of the negative emotions. Try taking a break from these people, or simply spending less time with them. If even then they still cause negativity, it may be time to cut them out completely.

CHAPTER 8

Plan For Success

ADHD is technically classified as a mental disorder. However, you may have noticed that I have refrained, as much as possible, from using that term throughout the book so far. That is because I see ADHD more as a variable in life, meant to make the equation a bit more interesting. And the best way to deal with this variable is to plan for it. How much ADHD impacts your life can be controlled by simply planning to succeed.

Reducing the Burden on Your Brain's Executive Functioning Skills

Your executive functioning skills are what allow you to perform tasks such as focusing, remembering, following instructions, planning your schedules, and multitasking successfully. This is one of the main areas of brain activity that are affected by ADHD and is one of the most important skills for life.

Luckily for us, technology has advanced quite well to take this into account and to help us make these tasks a lot easier. With technology placing the entire world at our fingertips, it comes as no surprise that we now have apps that can run on almost any smartphone to help to train and improve your executive functioning skills. This is a great way to help you to minimize some of the effects of ADHD.

In the interim, however, you still have to find a way to deal with daily life. Yet, technology has again thought of that and given us an answer. Every smartphone comes equipped with a few tools such as a calendar, an alarm clock, and even a virtual assistant. When you learn how to utilize these tools, you can take back control of your life.

Having your calendar at your fingertips is great for planning; you can immediately allocate your time efficiently and ensure that when you need to plan something you place it in your calendar immediately. This also helps you to refrain from double-booking.

Your alarm clock can serve several different purposes. It can remind you when you need to take breaks during the course of the day so that you can get your dopamine levels back up. It can also help you to schedule specific times during which you put away all distractions and only focus on your work. Knowing that this time will be well utilized, and then being able to take a break immediately afterward can help a lot with motivation and focus in your career, even more so if you use a progress-tracking app in conjunction with it.

Your virtual assistant, however, can be your most useful tool. This is almost like having another person to talk to and help keep you motivated. The functions a virtual assistant can perform are also ever-increasing.

The best way to find the apps to help you is to write down what executive functions you struggle with the most—for example, focusing on tasks at work. Then, doing a quick internet search for "apps to help me focus at work" will give you a wide variety of tools to help you in that specific area.

Developing Organizational Skills

Organizational skills are, perhaps, one of the main executive functions that people with ADHD struggle with, as well as one of the most important skills for success. This means that it is important to develop these skills. When you develop your organizational skills and implement them in your routine, especially at work, you'll see a definite improvement in your productivity. These skills can be hard to implement, so consider implementing them gradually over a period of time:

- **Clean and tidy your workspace:** When your workspace is

filled with clutter and objects that are not necessary for the task at hand, these objects will distract you quite easily. To clear these distractions from your mind, physically pack them away, and ensure that your workspace is neat and tidy, with as few distractions as possible—yet still stimulating and pleasant enough to keep you in a positive headspace.

- **Identify the goals you want to meet:** These goals extend all the way from your aspirations in life to your immediate goals on the task or project you are working on. Remember that some short-term goals will accumulate into reaching long-term goals. As long as your goals are clearly identified and you have a rough timeline in mind for when you want to reach them, you have taken your first giant step toward improving your organizational skills.

- **Create a to-do list for your goals:** A to-do list can be a great asset, especially when you use it to check off tasks you have already completed. This gives you a sense of progress and, in turn, helps to motivate you. Take your goals, and identify tasks that each goal needs in order to be achieved, these are the tasks you will add to your to-do list.

- **Prioritize the tasks on your to-do list:** Some tasks are dependent on other tasks to be completed first, and some tasks may take longer to complete than others. This means that you will need to identify what tasks are more important than others and assign them each their own priority. Think of it like baking. You use the oven only at the end of your recipe, but it needs to be at a certain temperature to use. At the same time, placing your mixture into an oven to bake is a very important aspect of the task. This is why most recipes start by telling you to switch the oven on at a certain heat. It is a high priority and lengthy task, so it is done first. Your own prioritization should mimic this.

- **Create a schedule for all your tasks:** The best way to ensure that you complete each task is to make a schedule for yourself. This can be a daily or weekly schedule that states when you will do each task and how long you have to complete the task. Although deadlines are difficult for us, giving yourself a reasonable one and trying to remain within it will really help you to be more motivated and remain focused for longer. You can also schedule breaks so that you are sure that you get enough time to refill your dopamine and energy levels.

- **Organize your space:** Although your space may be neat and tidy, it might still need to be organized—especially for someone working in an office environment or with an array of tools every day. By having your equipment well labeled and always in the same place, you save time and mental energy in finding them.

- **Reward yourself:** The goal is to keep your dopamine and energy levels high so that you can utilize them in focusing on your work. The best way to do so is through a reward system. Find something that you really enjoy—such as watching your favorite sports—and use this as your motivator. If you complete all your tasks in a day, or a major task, reward yourself with a ticket for the next game. You can also have smaller rewards for yourself during the course of the day such as something to snack on or playing a mission in your favorite game.

- **Balance your life:** This ties into your reward system. As someone with ADHD, if you expend all your energy on your work life, you will get burned-out very quickly. Similarly, if you allow your personal life to take priority you will always be distracted. Having hard boundaries—such as no working at home and no personal calls at work—allows you to balance your life and promotes your organizational skills.

Managing Time Blindness

Along with ADHD comes a little challenge called *time blindness*. What happens is that you become so focused on a certain task that you focus on nothing else. Before you know it, hours have passed and you feel like it's only been a few seconds. This, unfortunately, normally occurs when we are procrastinating or focusing on something completely irrelevant because that is when our mind relaxes.

There are a few steps that can help you manage your time blindness:

- **Know what causes time blindness:** Each of us has different activities that cause our time blindness. For some of us, it is playing a game. For others, it is scrolling social media, and for yet another, it could be just listening to the news. The first step to managing your time blindness is to find out which activities prompt it.

- **Set your alarms:** The main problem with time blindness is that it will often infringe on the times at which we are supposed to start doing meaningful and productive activities. We could start scrolling through our phones while on a break and completely miss the time we are supposed to go back to work. This is why setting an alarm is so important. This is a physical reminder of the time and can help to snap you out of your time blindness. You can also set multiple alarms, such as having an alarm ten minutes before you need to get back to work, another alarm five minutes before you have to get back to work, and then the last alarm at the exact time you have to get back to work. This way, you have time to prepare your own mindset, and you can allow yourself to indulge that procrastination feeling by ignoring two alarms while building a sense of urgency that will motivate you in time for the third alarm.

- **Outside help:** Sometimes, our time blindness is so soothing and good that we don't want to leave it. We ignore all our alarms and just keep going at it. If this happens to you often, you could always ask a friend, partner, or family member to call you just after your last alarm went off to make sure that you disengage from whatever activity has you stuck in the time blindness. Oftentimes, a little accountability is all you need to get yourself into gear.

- **Keep it interesting:** When we hear the same sound going off or we start the same activity at the same time of day every day, we easily get bored and just ignore it. So, make sure each alarm has its own completely distinct sound. The first one could just be a loud single note, the second could be a few notes as a gentle reminder, and the last could be a series of fast, loud sounds to promote urgency. Mixing it up will also help your brain wake up faster.

- **Break down your tasks:** When you wake up in the morning and you think about having to get ready for work, your mind realizes that this is at least 30 minutes if not longer that you will be busy doing a mundane task. If, however, you wake up and say to yourself, "Let's just get the shirt I want to wear today," that's a quick task that will be done in a few seconds. Stop thinking of only the bigger picture; it is sometimes good to look at the smaller tasks that make up the bigger picture so that you feel less overwhelmed.

- **Focus on a different time:** Instead of focusing on having to be at work by 9 a.m., start thinking about having to start getting ready at 7:30 a.m. When we think about the time that we are supposed to be at work, our brain decides that this is our deadline, so it will allow us to procrastinate until that time. If we change this and make an earlier time our deadline, we fool our brain into ensuring that we are on time.

- **Change your time:** There is another way to fool your brain into getting into gear earlier. Old analog clocks, especially ones that tick very loudly, are not just a reminder of every second that passes, but can also be made to lie about the time. By turning the hands forward 10 or even 30 minutes, you can lie to yourself about what the actual time is and, in that way, shock your brain awake much faster.

- **Overestimate problems:** Let's say the task you are about to complete is making dinner. It usually takes you about an hour and a half to make dinner from start to finish, try assuming that it will definitely take a bit longer. You might have trouble chopping the vegetables, or the meat might be somewhat thicker than it normally is, so it will take longer to prepare, or you could drop some of the food and have to start all over again. So, perhaps, you should start half an hour earlier, and give yourself two hours to complete dinner. You can always take your time when you see you'll have extra time or maybe even do something fancier or extra if you have spare time at the end.

- **Apps:** We've discussed apps earlier, but I would like to remind you of them again. There are many apps to help you stay on task and keep track of your time. A quick internet search will help you to easily find the right app for you.

- **Get some sleep:** One of the times we are most vulnerable to succumbing to time blindness is at night when we get into bed. It's very boring tossing and turning while waiting for sleep to come. So instead, we'll allow time blindness to overtake us until our body is physically too tired to continue working. Instead of doing this, hide away all your distractions, and try to force yourself into a healthy sleep schedule.

- **Plan time for planning:** Remember that planning is another one of the executive functioning skills that we struggle with. Yet, when we don't have our day and tasks planned out, it is a lot easier to allow our time blindness to take hold of us. So, make sure you schedule a time that you use specifically to update and create your next schedule.

- **Plan time for no plans:** If we create a constant schedule— one that always has us on the go and tells us exactly what we need to do and when—we start to feel a bit trapped. So, make sure that you have some time that you leave wide open. This is the time in which your impulsivity can take over and lead you to where the dopamine is. This also helps you feel a bit more free from your schedule.

Stress Management

Stress is a part of being human. We all experience it. We have demands from work, from our family, and even from ourselves. This all makes us tense up and stress, which leads to a vicious cycle of being unable to focus or sleep, constantly being anxious, body pains, depression, and the list goes on. Stress also shares quite a few side effects with ADHD. Unfortunately, this means that the shared effects these two conditions have on us become so much more severe.

As a result, we need to find ways to treat our stress as well as our ADHD. Since we're already looking at managing our ADHD, here are some ways to keep your stress levels down:

- Look for something positive to lift your mood.

- Accept that you can't control everything.

- Don't be aggressive. When you need to get your point or feelings across, do it in a clear and assertive way.

- Manage your time properly and effectively.

- Set boundaries and limitations on how far you can extend yourself, and don't feel bad saying no when you cannot handle more.

- Make time for yourself and your hobbies so that you can de-stress.

- Do not use alcohol or drugs for the purpose of relieving stress.

- Ask for support when you need it.

- Seek therapy if you could benefit from it.

You may have realized that the side effects of stress and ADHD are not the only similarities these two share. The treatments are quite similar as well, which means that you can sort out both at the same time. However, remember that if you suffer from both stress and ADHD, you will need to put extra effort into your ways of coping with them.

CHAPTER 9

Strengthening Your Mind

We've spoken about ways to work on your executive functioning skills quite quickly in the previous chapter. And although your executive functions (EFs) were at the core of planning for success, they were not the main focus. Now, we'll spend more time focusing on your EFs and how to strengthen your mind by addressing them.

Your EFs are the processes in your mind that basically affect your actions in your everyday life. In fact, your EFs are seen as more important to your success—in both academics and your career—than your IQ or socioeconomic status.

This means that maintaining healthy EFs is of the utmost importance. I want you to think of your EFs as a muscle that needs to constantly be exercised. If you stop exercising your muscles, they lose mass and become weaker, and the same happens with your EFs. If they are not constantly practiced and improved, they stagnate and become weak again.

By ensuring that your EFs are constantly on a trajectory of

improvement, you will also be able to help keep most of the effects of your ADHD in check. We'll be looking at the three core EFs, what parts of your life they impact, as well as activities to help improve them.

Inhibitory Control

The first EF we will be looking at is your *inhibitory control*. This can impact both your behavior and your attention. In the form of behavior, your inhibitory control determines how much self-control you have and what your responses to limitations will be.

This is the voice in your brain that is supposed to tell you that you should wait until after you finish your work before playing that game you just downloaded or that you shouldn't blurt out the first thing that comes into your mind. In essence, this is our impulse control. Of course, someone with ADHD does not have that voice in their mind telling them not to act on these impulses or give in to their inhibition. In children, this makes them look naughty, as if they don't care about what's right and what is wrong. In adults, it often makes us appear childish and as if we have no respect for rules or authority. In actual fact, what is happening is that the brain understands the behavior is wrong or the impulse should not be acted upon but does not know how not to refrain from doing it anyway.

When it comes to your inhibitory control, in regards to your attention, this influences your ability to ignore potential distractions and remain focused on the task at hand, regardless of how boring it is. Without this ability, you often appear uninterested or absentminded.

The best way to improve your inhibitory control is through turn-based interactions. Tabletop games are a great example of turn-based activities, but not all of us are interested in this. So, games such as golf or tennis where you have to wait for your turn to engage in the activity might be a better fit. If you have a child with ADHD, games like Simon Says will also help to strengthen their inhibitory control. Lastly, another activity that you may not realize helps you to strengthen your inhibitory control abilities is try-not-to-react challenges. These are challenges like trying not to laugh or not to sing along or dance to your favorite songs. By forcing yourself not to act on these impulses, you are strengthening your inhibitory control.

When it comes to the inhibitory control of your attention, activities such as listening to a podcast—where you have no other input aside from sound—help you to learn how to focus. If you force yourself to remain focused on this podcast, instead of becoming distracted by your work or any other action you may normally do, you are in fact strengthening your inhibitory control. You can also look at activities like juggling that require you to focus on a specific repetitive action. The longer you can continuously juggle, the healthier your attention and inhibitory control are.

Working Memory

The next EF we will be looking at is your *working memory*. This is the brain function used when you take in information, and you can manipulate and change this information as needed. A simple example would be accidentally hitting two stones together and seeing a spark fly from them, and then, hours later, upon seeing sparks from a flame meeting a piece of tinder, making the connection and using the stones and tinder to create your own flame.

This is a rudimentary explanation—as we all know how fire works—but it explains perfectly what working memory is. Your working memory is not just restricted to ideas. It is the use of any information that you can retain in your memory for a period of time and implement in other situations, such as following a list of instructions in the correct order to complete a task, remembering a question you would like to ask somebody while you wait for them to finish speaking, and so much more.

You can exercise your working memory by trying to mentally keep track of the total price of all your groceries while you are still shopping, through playing memory games, or even using a word-of-the-day calendar and making sure that you use the daily word at least three times throughout the day. Any activity that requires you to retain information and then implement it in different ways over a period of time will help you to improve your working memory.

Cognitive Flexibility

The third and last EF we will be looking at is called *cognitive flexibility*. This is your ability to change the way you think. When someone is "stuck in their ways," they lack cognitive flexibility. On the other hand, a healthy and well-practiced cognitive flexibility will allow you to adapt to change easily, view situations from different perspectives, more easily find solutions to problems, take advantage of unexpected opportunities, and admit that your viewpoint or opinion was indeed wrong when faced with new information.

The activities that allow you to improve your cognitive flexibility will be things like improv classes or freestyle dancing. Another exercise that you could do at any time and anywhere is to pick an object in front of you and find interesting ways that it shares commonalities with other objects in the room. For example, I have an orange cup next to me at the moment, and it is similar to the orange in my kitchen in the sense that they are both orange in color. It is similar to the vase on my desk since they both hold liquids, and it is similar to my printer since both of their exteriors are made from a plastic material.

All Executive Functions

Now that we have focused on each EF on its own, we can also note that there are activities that have the ability to improve each of these because they utilize all of them. Take cooking, for example: It improves your inhibitory control by making you do boring and repetitive tasks such as peeling potatoes. It improves your working memory by having you recall and follow a recipe step-by-step. It also improves your cognitive flexibility by making you think of the different ways you can cook and prepare your ingredients.

In addition to cooking, here is a list of just a few other activities which will help improve all three EFs:

- Music

- Dance

- Theater

- Sports

- Martial arts

- Camping

- Carpentry

- Animal care

Remember that your EFs are most impacted by your ADHD. By exercising them and continuously improving them, you are already treating your ADHD and finding a way to live with your diagnosis.

CHAPTER 10

Beyond Medications

Throughout the book so far, I've made mention of both therapeutic and medicinal treatments for ADHD. These, however, are not the only ways to treat your ADHD. But before we go any further, I would like to make it clear that therapy and medication are both *excellent* ways to treat your ADHD, and I encourage you to use both of these avenues. The methods and ideas below can and should be used in conjunction with your therapy and medication. I don't want you to think of these as an alternative treatment, but instead as extra tools to help enrich your life even further.

Riding the Wave

While we are on the subject of medication, I think that this would be the best time to discuss the impact that they have on you. I have no way of knowing what medication you are on or when you take it. What I do know, however, is that your medication will work in waves. Shortly after taking your medication, the wave will start reaching higher and higher as your brain chemistry levels out. Then, you will reach a peak where your brain chemistry is at optimal levels. The duration of this peak will be solely dependent on your treatment schedule. After a period of time, your brain chemistry will return to its own special norm.

Normally, your medication will be scheduled in a way that promotes a normal daily routine, so you will reach and try to maintain the peak of this wave during the middle of the day when you are most active. The rise will be while you wake up, and the drop as you are getting ready for bed.

The problem we face, however, is that when our medication is at a lower point, we tend to be more active and more easily distracted than we are when our medication is actually working. This is because our medication is specifically designed to allow our brains to combat our hyperactivity and impulsivity.

There is also the fact that your wave could be spread out over a few days instead of just one day. You will need to determine this wave cycle for yourself. So, why am I bringing this up? Because you need to adapt to this wave as well.

When you know what to expect from your wave, you will be better equipped to make the best of your highs and lows. When your medicine is working and you are at this peak of the wave, you should be focusing your time on your career and relationship. The aspects of your life that require your mental energy and emotional energy should be your highest priority at this time.

When the medication starts to wear off and you are at the lower ends of the wave, you will find yourself with more energy and distractions at hand. These are the times during which you should prioritize your free time and physical activities. You should allow yourself to be exhausted by getting rid of your excess energy and ensuring that you have the time and freedom to give in to your impulsivity.

When you learn and adapt to the highs and the lows, you will be able to make the most of your ADHD, turn the negatives into positives, challenges into opportunities, and show that your diagnosis just means you live life a bit differently, but no worse.

Complementary and Alternative Treatments

Complementary and alternative medicines (CAM) are treatments that are not generally seen as part of "Western" medicine. These treatments tend to focus more on your mind-body practices such as meditation, energy healing, massages, and natural products. These treatments can be used either with or instead of Western medicine. It is still, however, suggested that you consult your doctors and therapists before using any of these treatments, especially if you will be using them as an alternative treatment.

Recently, computer training programs and apps have also been proposed as ADHD treatments that will also form part of CAMs. These computer programs will target your EFs and, through specialized games and activities, attempt to alleviate the symptoms of ADHD.

Mindfulness Meditation

Some research has found that mindfulness meditation can help you to focus better and make your mind a bit calmer. Mindfulness meditation is where you observe the thoughts and feelings you have from moment to moment. The beauty of it is that it can be practiced while you are sitting, walking, or doing certain types of yoga.

The idea behind mindfulness meditation is to enter a meditative state by breathing slowly and adopting a nonjudgmental mindset. When you have entered this state, start by noticing the thoughts that pop into your mind. Perhaps, you can hear rain outside. Maybe, you can smell the residual scents of what you cooked earlier, and now it's making you hungry again. You might even find that all you can think is, "What am I supposed to be noticing? Oh, that was a thought! I noticed that!". I get it, starting to practice mindfulness feels clunky and awkward when your brain is used to being able to follow each thought at 1,000 miles per hour. That's normal, and it's okay. Just stick with it.

You don't need to do anything about the thoughts that come up. Just notice them, and let them go. It can be helpful to picture yourself writing each thought on a balloon and letting it float away. If you find that you are getting caught up in following a train of thought—rather than noticing your thoughts as a passive observer—simply bring yourself back to this visualization or to focusing on slowing your breathing. This practice serves to help us enhance our connection with our emotional selves and strengthens our ability to be aware of and respond to our own needs.

By engaging in a daily mindfulness meditation session of between five and fifteen minutes, you will train your mind to remain more focused on tasks, while also combatting depression and anxiety.

Energy Healing

Another CAM that we can look into is energy healing. The concept of energy healing is that the entire universe is made out of energy. Plants have energy, rocks, stones, and crystals all have energies, and we humans have our own energies as well.

These energies are always interacting with each other, and many factors can have an impact on the energy of something else in existence. Take the example I used earlier of striking two stones together to make a spark: The belief is that you used your energy to strike those stones. In turn, those stones' energies interacted with each other and created the spark.

This means that your ADHD forms part of your energy and that through your own actions and input from certain factors, you align your energy to better deal with your ADHD. By allowing your energy to flow unrestricted, the goal is to achieve the ability to do the following:

- Manage the stimuli

- Anchor your nervous system

- Engage with your life

When it comes to energy healing, however, there is no specific way of achieving your goal. There are many different paths that believe in energy healing, and each of these paths have their own ways of doing so. In Reiki, for example, this might be achieved by aligning your chakras and using certain crystals for their healing purposes, while in Wiccan paths, you might do a spell or ritual to achieve this.

If you want to try energy healing, you will need to research the countless different paths and methods available, find a practitioner in your area, and engage with them for specific guidance on how this can be achieved.

Conclusion

This book has been a journey for me. Every word and every page is filled with hours upon hours of research, and through this research, I have learned so much about myself, which makes me confident that you have as well.

The goal of this book has been to help you gain a better understanding of ADHD—whether you have been diagnosed or not. This book focuses on men with ADHD and the challenges they face, but I wanted to make sure that its information is accessible to everyone. Anyone should be able to pick up this book and understand the unique challenges that men face, especially when we receive a mental health diagnosis.

This diagnosis may not seem like much to the outside world, but therein lies the problem. It affects our lives on a daily basis, it affects our behaviors, and it creates many challenges for us that are often deemed as nothing. Although the world is changing and the conversation about men's mental health is finally starting to open up, there are still so many men that do not feel comfortable enough to discuss this very sensitive topic.

This is why here, in these pages, I have decided to address as much as I possibly can. We have opened up the conversation regarding our emotions. We have learned how to embrace and accept these emotions and to no longer be ashamed of them. They are, after all, an integral part of being human.

We've looked at the science and technical side of ADHD—how it impacts and changes our brain chemistry. ADHD actually causes our brains to create less happiness. That is the very simple truth of it, and in a time where suicide rates in men are on the rise, it is vitally important that we understand that men also need to learn how to regulate their emotions and what prohibits them from doing so.

We also need to accept our challenges because without acceptance we have no way to actually address them. We can follow every step of advice and every little guideline in this book, but as long as we do not accept the fact that we have ADHD, nothing will change. So if you have accepted it, you will now be able to rebuild once again.

By now, you should have already started implementing some of the advice in this book—advice such as how to improve your own self-esteem. You should have a healthier perspective in life that is no longer defined by your ADHD diagnosis. In fact, your sense of self-identity should never be determined by any diagnosis. You are a complete human being regardless of what label or diagnosis is placed on you.

Remember this the next time you are applying for a job or sitting in your office feeling more confident in your own abilities and seeing the possibilities of success that are laid out in front of you. Remember that you are in no way limited by your ADHD. Through careful planning, you can succeed in any aspect of your life, whether that is your career or your dating life.

Dating is challenging even without ADHD, but you have the guidelines now to ensure that your ADHD works to your benefit—to ensure that you make meaningful matches, whether online or in person, and that you will be able to communicate with confidence. Your perfect partner is out there waiting for you, and who knows, they may also have ADHD. You might even meet them while your chakras are being aligned.

This is now the time for me to say farewell, dear reader. May you achieve anything you set your mind to, and may you never worry another moment about your diagnosis. Remember, ADHD is just one small part of the great man that you already are.

References

Ansah, T. (2020, August 12). *Stages I Went Through Before Accepting My ADHD Diagnosis* HealthyPlace. https://www.healthyplace.com/blogs/livingwithadultadhd/2020/8/stages-i-went-through-before-accepting-my-adhd-diagnosis

Attention deficit hyperactivity disorder (ADHD). (2018b, May 30). *Overview - NHS.* https://www.nhs.uk/conditions/attention-deficit-hyperactivity-disorder-adhd/

Attention-Deficit / Hyperactivity Disorder (ADHD). (2018, October 11). Centers for Disease Control and Prevention. https://www.cdc.gov/ncbddd/adhd/index.html

Barkley, R. (2015, January 14). *What Is Executive Function? 7 Deficits Tied to ADHD.* ADDitude. https://www.additudemag.com/7-executive-function-deficits-linked-to-adhd/

Brit, J. (2019, December 12). *Organizational Skills: Definition and Examples* Indeed Www.indeed.com. https://www.indeed.com/career-advice/career-development/organizational-skills

Cherry, K. (2022, July 25). *What Is Self-Monitoring?* Verywell Mind. https://www.verywellmind.com/what-is-self-monitoring-5179838#:~:text=Self%2Dmonitoring%20is%20a%20personality

Diamond, A. (2022, February 24). *How to Sharpen Executive Functions: Activities to Hone Brain Skills.* ADDitude. https://www.additudemag.com/how-to-improve-executive-function-adhd/

Executive Function & Self-Regulation. (n.d.). Center on the Developing Child at Harvard University. https://developingchild.harvard.edu/science/key-concepts/executive-function/#:~:text=Executive%20function%20and%20self%2Dr egulation%20skills%20depend%20on%20three%20types

Fabello, M. A. (2016, May 26). *Dear Men: This Is How You Should Be Approaching a Woman on the Street.* Everyday Feminism. https://everydayfeminism.com/2016/05/men-approach-women-on-street/

Flanagan, C. (n.d.). *The 4 Questions That Can Defeat Negative Thoughts.* Oprah.com. Retrieved January 3, 2023, from https://www.oprah.com/omagazine/4-questions-that-defeat-negative-thoughts_1

Forness, A. (2019, December 7). *The Truth About Meeting People In Real Life Instead Of On Dating Apps.* Mindbodygreen. https://www.mindbodygreen.com/articles/meeting-people-in-real-life-without-using-dating-apps

General Prevalence of ADHD. (2018a). CHADD. https://chadd.org/about-adhd/general-prevalence/

How to Shift Your Perspective to Have a Positive Outlook. (2021, July 7). MasterClass. https://www.masterclass.com/articles/how-to-shift-your-perspective-to-have-a-positive-outlook

Ignorance breeds contempt, but knowledge breeds acceptance. [Tweet] (2023, January 22). *Twitter.* https://twitter.com/parraqiiii/status/1617028918455713793?t=NNp0ll1wz1YkURBf1eLJSw&s=08

Kinman, T., & Raypole, C. (2015). *ADHD vs. ADD: What's the Difference?* Healthline. https://www.healthline.com/health/adhd/difference-between-add-and-adhd

Kulman, R. (2014). *5 Must-Have Apps for Improving Executive Functioning in Children.* Beyondbooksmart.com. https://www.beyondbooksmart.com/executive-functioning-strategies-blog/5-great-apps-for-improving-executive-functioning-in-children

Leigh, J. (n.d.). *A story about ADHD: Self-healing & evolution.* Energy healing institute Retrieved January 10, 2023, from https://energyhealinginstitute.org/adhd-self-healing-evolution/

Levine, H. (2022, January 17). *Meditation and Yoga for ADHD.* WebMD. https://www.webmd.com/add-adhd/adhd-mindfulness-meditation-yoga#:~:text=One%20landmark%20UCLA%20study%20found

Marie, S. (2022, September 30). *Emotional Accountability: We Are Responsible for Our Own Feelings.* Psych Central. https://psychcentral.com/blog/we-are-responsible-for-our-own-feelings#recap

Megan. (2021, December 12). *5 Proven Ways to Stay Grounded (When Times Are Uncertain)!* Tracking Happiness. https://www.trackinghappiness.com/how-to-stay-grounded/

Mitchell, S. (2021, November 15). *Yes, Intentional Dating Is a Thing. Here's How To Do It Successfully.* Medium. https://betterhumans.pub/yes-intentional-dating-is-a-thing-heres-how-to-do-it-successfully-13d293464607

Montijo, S. (2022, March 31). *The Best Jobs for People with ADHD.* Psych Central. https://psychcentral.com/adhd/best-jobs-for-people-with-adhd

Mooney, J. (2022, January 16). *Accepting Your ADHD Diagnosis: Success with Attention Deficit.* Www.additudemag.com.

https://www.additudemag.com/adhd-myths-accept-diagnosis-success-story/

Nikki. (n.d.). *What It Looks Like To Accept Your ADHD*. Take Control ADHD. Retrieved January 1, 2023, from https://takecontroladhd.com/blog/category/what-it-looks-like-to-accept-your-adhd#:~:text=Accept%20%2D%20that%20ADHD%20is%20not

Nortje, A. (2020, April 3). *Realizing Your Meaning: 5 Ways to Live a Meaningful Life*. PositivePsychology.com. https://positivepsychology.com/live-meaningful-life/

Ragland, L. (2020, November 24). *Stress Management*. WebMD. https://www.webmd.com/balance/stress-management/stress-management

The Science of ADHD (2018b). CHADD. https://chadd.org/about-adhd/the-science-of-adhd/

7 Tips for Better Patience. Cleveland Clinic. (2019, January 16). https://health.clevelandclinic.org/7-tips-for-better-patience-yes-youll-need-to-practice/

Silver, L. (2006, November 30). *The ADHD Brain: Neuroscience Behind Attention Deficit*. ADDitude. https://www.additudemag.com/adhd-neuroscience-101/

Song, Y. (2020). *10 Tips for Maintaining a Healthy Lifestyle and Body Weight*. , Fairbanks School of Public Health. https://fsph.iupui.edu/doc/10-Tips-Healthy-Lifestyle.pdf

Symptoms - Attention deficit hyperactivity disorder (ADHD).(2018a). NHS. https://www.nhs.uk/conditions/attention-deficit-hyperactivity-disorder-adhd/symptoms/

Tartakovsy, M. (2019, January 4). *How to Ask Your Spouse for Support—Without Sounding Like a Nag or Critic*. Psych Central.

https://psychcentral.com/lib/how-to-ask-your-spouse-for-support-without-sounding-like-a-nag-or-critic#8

10 Ways How to Overcome Challenges Life Throws at You. (2020, March 30). University of the People. https://www.uopeople.edu/blog/10-ways-how-to-overcome-challenges/

10 Ways to Improve Your Communication Skills. (n.d.). Talent Solutions Right Management. https://manpowergroup.com/wcm/connect/right-it-it/legacy-home/thoughtwire/categories/career-work/10-Ways-to-Improve-Your-Communication-Skills

Tuckman, A. (2022, January 3). *12 Ways to Stop Wasting Time.* Www.additudemag.com. https://www.additudemag.com/slideshows/stop-wasting-time/#:~:text=Alarms%20are%20a%20simple%2C%20effective

Understanding ADHD: Complementary and Alternative Treatment of ADHD. (n.d.). Health.ucdavis.edu. Retrieved January 10, 2023, from https://health.ucdavis.edu/mindinstitute/research/about-adhd/adhd-cam-treatments.html

Watson, S. (2022, August 25). *ADHD in the Workplace.* WebMD. https://www.webmd.com/add-adhd/adhd-in-the-workplace

What does it mean to truly accept your ADHD brain?. (n.d.). Bmindful. Retrieved January 1, 2023, from https://bmindful.ca/acceptance-and-adhd/

What's the difference between mental health and mental illness?. (2015). Canadian Mental Health Association, BC Division. *Here to Help.* https://www.heretohelp.bc.ca/q-and-a/whats-the-difference-between-mental-health-and-mental-illness

Wooll, M. (2021, July 22). *Be brave even if you aren't yet (9 ways to conquer your fears).* Betterup Www.betterup.com. https://www.betterup.com/blog/how-to-be-brave

Zauderer, S. (2022, November 14). *How Many People Have ADHD? 45 ADHD Statistics*. Crossriver Therapy Www.crossrivertherapy.com. https://www.crossrivertherapy.com/adhd-statistics